South Park

Jose Escobar

FADE IN:

Very happy, Disneyesque MUSIC swirls in.

PAN DOWN from a pretty blue sky, to a small quaint town nestled in the hills. A wooden sign tells us this is South
Park.

EXT. SOUTH PARK AVENUE - DAY

Birds fly into the air, TOWNSPEOPLE smile to each other as they walk by.

It is a scene reminiscent of, if not directly ripped off from, the opening number of 'Beauty and the Beast'.

A little eight year old boy walks happily down the street. He is STAN MARSH, a noble looking boy with piercing blue eyes and a strong chin. As he walks, he sings a happy song.

STAN

I'm going to the movies
To see the brighter side of life!
I'm going to the movie
Everything's gonna be alright!
Forget all my troubles
Put my own life on hold
Let a studio tell me how I should view the world
Where everything works out
I love it that way
I'm going to the movies
The movies today!

Stan merrily walks up to a crappy looking house.

INT. BEDROOM - MORNING

We are in a young boy's bedroom, just as his alarm clock goes off. BRRRRRTTT!!!

RADIO ANNOUNCER

Good morning South Park! It's five-thirty a. m. on Sunday!! Time to feed the horses and water the cows!!

From the back, we see the blond haired kid sit up from his bed. He stretches, and then walks over to his closet.

We still only see the boy from the back as he reaches in his closet and pulls out an orange coat.

The kid puts his coat on, then turns to camera and pulls the hood shut, so that we never get a good look at his face.

MOTHER (O. S.)

KENNY! YOU'RE GONNA BE LATE FOR CHURCH!!!
This boy's name is KENNY, and under his orange coat, we have no idea what he looks like, except for his European nose and hazel eyes.

KENNY
Mph rmph rm!

INT. KENNY'S HOUSE - KITCHEN
Kenny walks through his small, dirty house and into the kitchen, where his MOTHER, FATHER and OLDER BROTHER are sitting at the humble table.

KENNY'S MOTHER
Sit down, you can share some of your brother's waffle.
The doorbell rings. Kenny walks over to the door.

EXT. KENNY'S HOUSE - DAY
Kenny opens the door to find Stan.

STAN
Kenny! The Terrance and Phillip movie is out! You wanna come?!
Stan shows Kenny a newspaper clipping. It's an ad for the new
Terrance and Phillip movie 'Asses of fire'. Kenny's eyes light up

KENNY
Mph rmph rm, rmph!
Kenny walks away with Stan. His mother comes out after him.

KENNY'S MOTHER
Kenny! Where're you going?

KENNY
Mph mprh mprh rm!

KENNY'S MOTHER
What do you mean you don't want to go to church?

KENNY
Mrmph, rmph rmph rm rmph.
Kenny and Stan walk down the street.

KENNY'S MOTHER
Well fine, go ahead and miss church!! And then when you die and go to hell you can
ANSWER TO SATAN!!

Dramatic MUSIC STING. Kenny stops, thinks for a minute... And then walks off with Stan anyway.

EXT. SOUTH PARK AVENUE - DAY
Stan and Kenny now both happily march down the street to the happy beat.
TOM, a plastic surgeon, peeps his head out the door of his
Rhinoplasty office.

TOM
Say, where are you boys going?

STAN
We're going to the movies!
To see the brighter side of life!
Where everyone is beautiful
And have their hair combed just right!

KENNY
Mph rmph rm rmph rm!
Mph rm rmph rm!
Mprh rm rmph rm rm
Rmph rm rmph rm rmph!

TOM
Have fun you rascals!

EXT. KYLE'S HOUSE - DAY
Kenny and Stan knock at the door.
A handsome eight year old Semite, KYLE, answers the door.

KYLE
Hey, dudes... Aren't you supposed to go to church, Kenny?

STAN
Kyle, check it out.
Kenny holds up the newspaper clipping.

KYLE
OH MY GOD, DUDE!!!
Kyle slips on his coat and heads out the door. But just then,
Kyle's little brother, IKE, a two year old adopted Canadian boy bounces up next to him.

KYLE

4

No, Ike! You can't come with me!
Kyle's MOTHER, a big fat bitch, comes to the door and yells.

KYLE'S MOTHER
Kyle, you take your little brother out to play with you!

KYLE
Aw, ma!!

KYLE'S MOTHER
Do as I say, Kyle!
Kyle's mother closes the door.

KYLE
Damn it!!

EXT. SOUTH PARK AVENUE - DAY
Now the three boys, and little Ike, merrily strut down the street and sing in unison.

BOYS
We're going to the movies
To see the better side of life
Where something interesting happens
Every day and night!

KYLE
In movies we can pretend
That love is real and good always wins-

STAN
We can even make believe marriages last!
A HOMELESS guy is lying in the alley.

HOMELESS GUY
Spare a dollar? Spare a dollar?
Stan walks by and throws a dollar at him. The homeless guy suddenly jumps up.

HOMELESS GUY
I'm going to the movies!
To see the brighter side of life!
I'm going to the movies
Everything's gonna be alright!
Forget my troubles

Put my own life on hold
Let a studio tell me how to view the world!

KYLE
Let's go get fat ass!

EXT. ANOTHER HOUSE - DAY
This house looks just like all the others.

INT. THAT SAME HOUSE
CLOSE UP on a bag that reads 'CHEESY POOFS'. A hand reaches into the bag, pulls out a wad of orange crunchies and raises them --
BOOM UP to reveal the fat face of eight year old ERIC CARTMAN who chows down on the chips.
Now we see that fat little Eric is sitting on his couch, eating Cheesy Poofs and watching television.
The doorbell rings. Cartman doesn't move a muscle.

CARTMAN
MOM! SOMEBODY'S AT THE DOOR!
CARTMAN'S MOTHER enters. She is extremely June Cleaveresque
(except that she's a hermaphrodite crack whore). She returns with Stan, Kyle and Kenny.

CARTMAN'S MOTHER
Look, Eric it's your little friends.

CARTMAN
What the hell are you guys doing here?

IKE
Baba turtre bad!
Kyle holds up the newspaper ad.

CARTMAN
Ooh!

EXT. SOUTH PARK AVENUE
Now all four boys are merrily walking down the street and singing.

BOYS
We're going to the movies
To see the better side of life!

CARTMAN
Maybe there'll be pirates!
Or a whole city burnin'!
Maybe we'll see a monster
Or, better yet, Uma Thurman!

BOYS
We're going to the movies!
Everything's gonna be okay!
The boys skip out of frame.

EXT. MOVIE THEATRE - DAY
The movie theatre is nestled neatly between two other South
Park buildings.
The boys walk up to the geeky, teenage TICKET GUY.

BOYS
Going to the movies!
The movies today!!!!!

STAN
Can I get five tickets to Terrance and
Phillip Asses of Fire, please?

TICKET GUY
No.
Suddenly, all the happy music that has permeated the film comes to an ABRUPT HALT.
The boys look confused.

KYLE
What'dya mean, no?

TICKET GUY
Terrance and Phillip Asses of Fire is rated 'R'. You kids can't get in.
The boys look shocked. They just stand there, in silence.

CARTMAN
The hell we can't! My money is just as good as any white person's!

TICKET GUY
You have to be accompanied by a parent or guardian.

KYLE

But why?

TICKET GUY
Because this movie has naughty language, and it might make you kids start using bad words.

CARTMAN
Listen you son of a bitch, if you don't let us in to see this movie I'm gonna kick you square in the nuts.

TICKET GUY
Sorry, Charlie.

KYLE
Damn it!

TICKET GUY
Next, please?
A few TEENAGERS walk up to get their tickets. The boys step aside.

STAN
This is terrible! This can't be happening!!

KYLE
We HAVE to see this movie, dude!

CARTMAN
Aw, screw it. It probably isn't all that good anyway.

KYLE
Cartman! What the hell are you talking about?! You LOVE Terrance and Philiip!

CARTMAN
Yeah, but the animation's all crappy - it probably can't sustain itself over ninety minutes.

IKE
Poo baba!

STAN
Wait! I've got an idea!

EXT. MOVIE THEATRE - A LITTLE LATER
The old Homeless guy from the intro song walks up to the

8

Ticket Guy with the boys.

HOMELESS GUY
Uh, hi. I want five tickets to Terrance and Phillip Asses of Fire.

TICKET GUY
You realize this movie is rated R? It may not be appropriate for your little ones.

HOMELESS GUY
Oh.
(Turning to boys)
Hey, he says this movie isn't appropriate for you.

STAN
(Whispering)
Look, homeless guy, if you don't want to buy us tickets, and NOT get your ten bucks and NOT go buy yourself a bottle of
Vodka and not forget about how miserable your life is and not stop the voices in your head then go right ahead.

HOMELESS GUY
Five tickets please.
The Ticket guy suspiciously hands them over.

INT. MOVIE THEATER - DAY
The boys are all sitting in the front row. Cartman has a huge tub of popcorn, all kinds of candy, and a large drink.

IKE
Purpre mama!

KYLE
Be quiet, Ike! The movie's starting!

ANGLE - MOVIE SCREEN
A TITLE reads 'Terrance and Phillip - Asses of Fire'

BOYS
HOORAY!!!
On the screen, we come across PHILLIP, a very handsome
Canadian star with a great body.

PHILLIP

9

Say Terrance, what did the Spanish Priest say to the Uranian gynecologist?
PAN OVER to TERRANCE, who is also Canadian, and equally handsome in a more rugged way.

TERRANCE
I don't know, Phillip, what?
Phillip rips a big fart. Terrance and Phillip laugh merrily.

ANGLE - BOYS
Laughing their asses off.

KYLE
That was sweet!

STAN
Where do they come up with this stuff?!

CARTMAN
How come Terrance and Phillip are so weird looking?

KYLE
Cuz, dummy they're Canadian, just like
Ike!

CARTMAN
Oh.

IKE
Poo bada!

ANGLE - SCREEN
TERRANCE
You're such a pigfucker, Phillip!

PHILLIP
What?! Why would you call me a pigfucker?!

TERRANCE
Well, let's see... First of all, you fuck pigs.

PHILLIP
Oh yeah!
Terrance and Phillip laugh merrily.

ANGLE - BOYS
KYLE
Woa, dude! Did they say what I think they said?

ANGLE - SCREEN
Terrance pulls out a white envelope.

TERRANCE
Well, fuck my ass and call me a bitch, I just got a letter!

PHILLIP
A letter from who, you shit sucking cock master?
TRACK IN on the boys' wide eyed faces as the dialogue from the film enters their innocent ears.

TERRANCE
It's from your mother.

PHILLIP
My mother sent YOU a letter? What's it say?

TERRANCE
It says 'Dear Terrance, please don't ever tell my son that I licked your hairy balls. '
Terrance and Phillip laugh merrily.

PHILLIP
Oh, you fucking ball whore!
The boys don't laugh, they just smile widely, they seem busy taking it all in.

CARTMAN
Wow... Ball whore...

TERRANCE
Listen, you donkey raping shit eater-

KYLE
(To himself)
Donkey raping shit eater.

IKE
Doky maping she deeder!!!

TERRANCE
You'd fuck your uncle!

PHILLIP
YOU'D fuck your uncle!

TERRANCE
(Singing)

Shut your fucking face,
Unclefucka!!
You're an asslicking, Ball sucking
Unclefucka!!
You're an Unclefucka, yes it's true
Nobody fucks Uncles quite like you-

PHILLIP
SHUT YOUR FUCKING FACE!!
UNCLEFUCKA!!!
YOU'RE the one that fucked your
Uncle, UNCLEFUCKA!!!
You don't eat, or sleep or mow the lawn
You just fuck your Uncle all day long!

TERRANCE & PHILLIP
Shut your fucking face, Unclefucka!
You butt licking bastard
Unclefucka!

TERRANCE
You're an Unclefucka I must say!

PHILLIP
You fucked YOUR Uncle yesterday!

TERRANCE & PHILLIP
Unclefucka! That's YOUUUUUUU!!!!!
The song ends and the boys erupt into applause.

EXT. MOVIE THEATRE - DAY
The boys walk out of the theatre with glazed eyes and wide smiles.

KYLE

Dude, that movie was fucking sweet!

CARTMAN
You bet your fucking ass it was!

STAN
Fuck, dude, I wanna be just like Terrance and Phillip!

TICKET GUY
Hey wait a minute... Where's your guardian?

STAN
Huh?

TICKET GUY
I knew it! You PAID a homeless guy to get you in, didn't you!
The boys think a second.

CARTMAN
Suck my balls.

KYLE
Yeah,
(Singing)

Shut your fucking face,
Unclefucka!!
The boys walk away, merrily. The ticket guy is in shock.

TICKET GUY
Oh oh, I'm in trouble.

BOYS
(Singing, fading off)

You're an asslicking, ball sucking
Unclefucka!!

EXT. STARK'S POND - DAY
All the children of South Park are gathered at the pond for ice skating.
The scene is reminiscent of the skating scene from the
Charlie Brown Christmas special.
Delicate snowflakes fall, children laugh and skate, and joyous music plays.

The boys walk up to the pond.

CLYDE
Hey, where have you guys been all day?

STAN
Oh, nowhere... We just went out to go see the TERRANCE AND PHILLIP MOVIE!
All the kids gasp! Dramatic MUSIC STING.

BEBE
You saw it?!

CLYDE
How'd you get in?!
Suddenly, all the kids are gathered around the boys. They're like celebrities.

CARTMAN
Hey! Stop crowding us you shitfaced cockmasters!
All the kids stop, wide eyed. As if they've just hear the voice of God.

KIDS
Wowwww...

STAN
Yeah, you're all a bunch of ass ramming unclefuckers.

KIDS
Ooooohhh!!!

CLYDE
(To another kid)
We HAVE to see this movie, dude.
The other kids nod.

CARTMAN
Hey Stan, tell 'em about when Terrance called Phillip a testicle shitting rectal wart! Stan?
Stan?
But Stan is elsewhere, because out on the ice, skating gracefully, is little eight year old
WENDY TESTABURGER.
The heavens part, a CHOIR OF ANGELS sing, as Wendy skates around and around,
performing a series of impossible Triple
Lutzes, Sowcows and what-have-you-not's.
All the animals of the forest -- deer, birds, bunnies -- all stop to admire her.

Stan's smile grows wider and wider. Kyle turns to see what he's looking at.

STAN
Thank my lucky stars
Here before me now
Is everything I'd ever hoped for
Knew it in a word
Saw it in a glance
The only thing I think I'd die for...

KYLE
Aw, God Damn it, he's singing that fucking song again.

ANGLE - WENDY
Spinning and soaring in slo-mo. Effortlessly covering every inch of the pond with her ballet maneuvers.
Stan is slack-jawed.

STAN
I can't stop now
My heart's awake
I pray her arms my arms to take
So this is why I'm ali-
Wendy finishes her routine with a triumphant Hamill-camel landing right in front of Stan and spraying ice in his face and abruptly ending his song.

WENDY
Hi, Stan!
Stan vomits profusely all over himself.

WENDY
Ew! Gross!
Just then, another kid skates up, spraying more ice in Stan's face. His name is GREGORY, and he is a very handsome eight year old boy, with golden hair and an open-buttoned shirt. He speaks with a rich English accent.

GREGORY
Come, Wendy, let us try to jump the hilly brush.
Stan looks at Gregory.

STAN
Who are you, kid?

GREGORY
My name is Gregory. I have been Wendy's counter-cousin for some time.

WENDY
Want to skate with us?

GREGORY
We've been skating all morning. And laughing and talking of memories past.
Gregory skates away. Stan looks stunned. Finally, he tries to get Wendy's attention.

STAN
We saw the Terrance and Phillip movie!

WENDY
That's nice, Stan.
Wendy skates after Gregory. Stan looks completely rejected.

KYLE
Woa, dude, who's your girlfriend's new guy?

STAN
She's not my girlfriend, dude!
Meanwhile, the schoolkids are all still gathered around
Cartman.

CARTMAN
Yes, I saw the Terrance and Phillip movie. Who wants to touch me? I said,
"Who wants to touch me?!"
A small boy steps forward and tentatively touches Cartman's arm.

SMALL BOY
Oooooh...

EXT. SOUTH PARK - TOWN - MORNING
Establishing shot of the little town of South Park which consists of four buildings. The
sun rises in the background.
It's a brand new day.

EXT. SOUTH PARK ELEMENTARY - DAY
The elementary school is nestled peacefully between two mountain peaks.

INT. SOUTH PARK ELEMENTARY - DAY
The kids of South Park are all in their seats, singing.

KIDS
Shut your fucking face,
Unclefucka!!
You're a shitsucking, cocksucking
Unclefucka!!
The door opens, and suddenly the kids quiet down.
CLOSE-UP on a hand puppet with a large red hat. It seems to be speaking.

MR. HAT
Okay, children, let's take our seats.
As the voice continues, we PULL BACK to reveal that the puppet is on the right hand of MR. GARRISON, a forty-six year old teacher who is in denial about his homosexuality.

MR. GARRISON (AS MR. HAT)
We have a lot to learn and precious little time.
Garrison looks over the class and notices that every single one of them is wearing a Terrance and Phillip T-shirt, except, of course, for Wendy.

MR. GARRISON
Why is everyone wearing T-shirts of
Sigfried and Roy?

KYLE
It's not Sigried and Roy, Mr. Garrison, it's Terrance and Phillip.

KIDS
TERRANCE AND PHILLIP!!
Stan looks over at Wendy. She just rolls her eyes. Stan sulks.

MR. GARRISON
Well, anyway... Today children, our friend Mr. Hat is going to tell us all about the environment.

MR. GARRISON (AS MR. HAT)
That's right, Mr. Garrison. The environment is what surrounds us. It is what we live and breathe.

CARTMAN
I hate the environment.

KYLE
Dude, how can you hate the environment?

CARTMAN
'Cuz, dude, it's all sticky and airy and fragile and stuff. I fucking hate it.
The kids all GASP!

MR. GARRISON
Eric! Did you just say the "F" word?

CARTMAN
Fragile?

KYLE
No, he's talking about fuck, dude. You can't say fuck in front of Mr. Garrison.

MR. GARRISON
Kyle!

CARTMAN
Why the fuck not?

MR. GARRISON
Eric!

STAN
Dude, you just said fuck again.

MR. GARRISON
Stanly!

KENNY
Mph.

MR. GARRISON
Kenny!

CARTMAN
That's bullshit! If Terrance and Phillip can say something, I should be able to say it too!

BEBE
Wow, Cartman's cool!

CLYDE
He's like Terrance and Phillip!

Cartman gloats proudly.

CARTMAN
Fuckin' a right.

MR. GARRISON
How would you like to go to the principal's office?

CARTMAN
How would you like to gargle rat jiz?
Mr. Garrison is in shock.

MR. GARRISON
WHAT DID YOU SAY?!?!
CARTMAN
I said -
Cartman takes out a megaphone, hits the switch and puts it to his mouth. It feeds back horribly.

CARTMAN
(Through megaphone)

HOW WOULD YOU LIKE TO GARGLE RAT JIZ?!
Garrison is floored.

KYLE
Oh, dude we are fucked now.

INT. PRINCIPAL'S OFFICE - DAY
The boys are seated in front of the Principal's desk.

STAN
Now remember, don't tell anybody we saw the Terrance and Phillip movie!

KYLE
Yeah, let's swear we won't tell!
Just then, the Principal walks in. She is PRINCIPAL VICTORIA, a frizzy haired woman of about forty.

PRINCIPAL VICTORIA
I am VERY disappointed in you boys!
You should be ASHAMED of yourselves! I've already called in your parents, but first I want you to THINK about what you've done.

CARTMAN
Principal Victoria, can I ask a question?

PRINCPAL VICTORIA
What?

CARTMAN
What's the big fucking deal?

STAN
Yeah.

PRINCIPAL VICTORIA
AGH!! I want to know where you heard these horrific obscenities!
The boys look at each other.

STAN
Nowhere.

KYLE
I'VE heard them from Mr. Garrison a few times before...

STAN
Yeah!

PRINCIPAL VICTORIA
Boys, I seriously doubt that Mr. Garrison ever said-
(Reading)
'Eat penguin shit you cum sucking ass spelunker' in school!
The boys all laugh.
But then the door opens and in walks Stan's mother, Kyle's mother, Cartman's mother and
Kenny's mother.

STAN
Oh, oh...

PRINCIPAL VICTORIA
Thank you all for coming on such short notice. As you can see, your boys are all being
disciplined.

STAN'S MOTHER
This just isn't like you, Stanley!

Stan looks down at the floor.

KYLE'S MOTHER
What did my son say, Principal Victoria?
Did he say the S word?

PRINCIPAL VICTORIA
No, it was worse than that...

KYLE'S MOTHER
(Gasping)
The F word?!

PRINCIPAL VICTORIA
No, worse. Here's a short list of the things they've been saying.
The mothers look over the sheet of paper. Immediately, their eyes bulge.

STAN'S MOTHER
Oh dear God...

KYLE'S MOTHER
What is 'fisting'?

CARTMAN'S MOTHER
That's when the fist is inserted into the anus or vagina for sexual pleasure.
The two moms stare at Ms. Cartman.

CARTMAN'S MOTHER
What?

KYLE'S MOTHER
(To Kyle)
Young man, you will tell Peincipal
Victoria THIS INSTANT where you heard all these horrible phrases!

KYLE
I can't dude! We all took a sacred oath, and swore ourselves to secrecy!

CARTMAN
It was the Terrance and Phllip movie!

STAN
Dude!

CARTMAN
What? Fuck you guys, I wanna get out of here.

KYLE'S MOTHER
Terrance and Phillip MOVIE?! Oy gevalt!
Not again!

PRINCIPAL VICTORIA
What is Terrance and Phillip?

KYLE'S MOTHER
Terrance and Phillip are two VERY untalented, unfunny actors from Canada.
Their TV show is filled with toilet humor and bad language and is just complete garbage.
Now it appears they have a movie and I'm positive it's not suitable for children!

PRINCIPAL VICTORIA
Well, it looks like I'll have to send a warning letter out to parents. I have to put a stop to
this before MORE children see 'Terrance and Phillip'.

CARTMAN
Everybody's already fucking seen it.

MS. CARTMAN
Eric!

CARTMAN
I'm sorry! I can't help it!! That movie has warped my fragile little mind.

KYLE'S MOTHER
Alright, boys, that's enough. Get out and let us adults speak.
The boys get up and walk out. Kyle's mother slams the door behind them.

KYLE'S MOTHER
We must take action on this immediately.

PRINCIPAL VICTORIA
Ooh yes. I think we'll have to give detention to those boys.

KYLE'S MOTHER
Forgive me for saying so, Principal
Victoria, but your methods are too...
Shall we say... soft? As head of the

PTA, I am exercising my right under article 42 of the PTA code.
A look of shock comes over the principal's face.

PRINCIPAL VICTORIA
Article 42! You don't mean-?!

KYLE'S MOTHER
Yes Principal Victoria. The PTA is impeaching you.

PRINCIPAL VICTORIA
But I-

KYLE'S MOTHER
You are officially relieved of your duties as principal of this school!
Kyle's mother sits herself down at Principal Victoria's desk.

KYLE'S MOTHER
Get out of that chair! The PTA is in charge now!

INT. CAFETERIA - DAY
The other school kids are in line for lunch.
Just then, the Kyle's mother's voice comes blaring through the P. A.

KYLE'S MOTHER
Attention students. We are now enforcing a new dress code at South Park
Elementary. Terrance and Phillip shirts are NO LONGER ALLOWED IN SCHOOL.
Anyone wearing a Terrance and Phillip shirt is to be SENT HOME IMMEDIATELY.
The kids look down. They're all wearing Terrance and Phillip shirts.

KIDS
HOOORAY!!!
The kids all cheer and run out the door. Leaving the cafeteria absolutely empty... Except
for Wendy.

WENDY
Hello?
Wendy's hello echoes throughout the entire building.

INT. TELEVISION SET
A dapper NEWS ANCHOR sits behind a news desk.

NEWS ANCHOR
All over America, kids are flocking to the R rated film, 'Terrance and Phillip

Asses of Fire'. Here with a special report, is a quadriplegic midget in a bikini.

INT. SPELLING BEE - DAY
A QUADRIPLEGIC MIDGET IN A BIKINI stands in front of the camera with a microphone.

Q. MIDGET W/BIKINI
Thanks, Tom. It appears that the effects of the Canadian Comedy are far reaching indeed. All over America, children seem to be influenced.
A TEACHER is on stage with a young spelling bee contestant.

TEACHER
Alright, this is for the silver medal.
Spell 'Forensics'.

KID
Oh, fuck that, why should I fucking have to spell forensics?
All the kids cheer.

KID
Here you go; S-U-C-K-M-Y-A-S-S,

FORENSICS.
CUT TO:
EXT. BIRTHDAY PARTY - DAY
A happy birthday party is going on is some kids backyard. A clown is entertaining everyone.

CLOWN
Hey kids, how would you like to see some magic tricks?!

KIDS
FUCK YOU!!
The clown looks startled.

CLOWN
Huh?

CHILD
Yeah, and fuck your stupid little red nose.

CHILD 2
Yeah, and fuck your yellow hair. And fuck your gay pants.

PAN OVER to again find the midget reporter. He now has a graphic of a record chart next to him.

Q. MIDGET W/BIKINI
And the devastating impact of the
Canadian phenomenon is Terrance and
Phillip's new hit song, "Shut Your
Fucking Face, Unclefucka" which has climbed the charts with a bullet --
We see a clip from the video, "Unclefucka. "
The video has Terrance and Phillip dressed like Mase and
Puffy in that video they did in Vegas. They wear shiny bright jumpsuits and lunge at the fish-eye lens of the camera.

TERRANCE & PHILLIP
(Singing)

Shut your fucking face!
Unclefucka!!

INT. NEWSROOM - DAY
The news anchor shakes his head in disgust.

NEWS ANCHOR
Thanks, midget. Shocking report. The controversy surrounding the Terrance and
Phillip movie began in the small mountain town of South Park, Colorado where the local
PTA banned the movie. With us tonight is the head of the South Park
PTA, Sheila Brofloski-
A screen appears with Kyle's mother, looking very pissed. The
TITLE below her reads 'Outraged Mother'.

NEWS ANCHOR
Ms. Brovlofski, how are these kids seeing this film? Is bad parenting to blame? Or is it
Canada?

KYLE'S MOTHER
Canada!

NEWS ANCHOR
Alright. Here with a counterpoint is the
Canadian Minister of Movies.
A split screen appears, Kyle's mother on one side, and a goofy looking Canadian slides
into the other.

NEWS ANCHOR
Thank you, Minister, for joining us.

CANADIAN MINISTER OF MOVIES
Thanks for having me, buddy.

NEWS ANCHOR
Minister, parents all over America are concerned about your country's entertainment. Your thoughts?

CANADIAN MINISTER OF MOVIES
Well, the film is R rated, and it's not intended for children-

KYLE'S MOTHER
Oh but OF COURSE children are going to see it!!

CANADIAN MINISTER OF MOVIES
Uh, can I finish? Can I finish? ... The fact is that we Canadians are quite surprised by your outrage-

KYLE'S MOTHER
YOU JUST DON'T CARE!
CANADIAN MINISTER OF MOVIES
Can I finish? Hello? Can I finish? ... The
United States has graphic images of violence on television all the time, what is that one show? COPS? And car crashes caught on tape? We can't believe that a movie with some foul language and fart jokes would piss you off so much.

KYLE'S MOTHER
BECAUSE IT'S EVIL!!
CANADIAN MINISTER OF MOVIES
Can I finish? Please? Can I finish? ...
... Uh... Okay, I'm finished.

NEWS ANCHOR
But minister, it isn't like this film is the first troublesome thing to come out of Canada. Let us not forget Brian Adams a few decades ago.
The Minister thinks.

CANADIAN MINISTER OF MOVIES
What?

KYLE'S MOTHER

The Canadians are just mad that we mothers here in South Park have the chutzpah to stand up to them! Like it or not, Mr. Canadian Minister, OUR children are now safe from your Canadian smut!

INT. MOVIE THEATRE - DAY
The boys are in the front row, this time with Wendy, watching the Terrance and Phillip movie.

TERRANCE
Well, Terrance I hope you learned something from this whole experience.

PHILLIP
I did, Terrance, I learned that you are a boner biting dick fart fuck face!
The boys laugh merrily. Wendy just looks bored.

TERRANCE
Say Phillip, want to see the Northern
Lights?

PHILLIP
You bet, Terrance!
Terrance pulls out a match, lights it, then farts.
The flame burns Terrance to a blackened mass.

PHILLIP
HA HA HA! You burned yourself to death by lighting the fart! HA HA HA!!

TERRANCE
(Just a skull)
I sure did, Phillip!!
The boys laugh hysterically.

STAN
Did you see that, Wendy?

WENDY
Yup.

EXT. THEATER - DAY
The boys walk out happily.

KYLE
Man, that movie gets better every time I see it!

CARTMAN
Yeah, but you know what? That whole part about lighting farts is bullshit. You can't do that.

KENNY
Mph rmpmh rm.

CARTMAN
No way.

STAN
Didn't you think it was funny, Wendy?

WENDY
Stan... I think you and I need some time apart.

STAN
WHAT?!

CARTMAN
Oh shit.

WENDY
It's just... It's obvious that we don't have a whole lot in common anymore. I need somebody who's... a little deeper.

STAN
But Wendy, I can go-
Wendy places her little gloved hand over Stan's mouth.

WENDY
No. Don't speak. You'll only make things more annoying. Goodbye, Stan.
And just like that, Wendy is gone. Stan looks almost ready to cry.
Kyle walks up behind Stan.

KYLE
Dude, anybody who doesn't think Terrance and Phillip is funny can fuck off anyways.

STAN
(Insincere)
Yeah...
The boys walk off.

KENNY
Mph rmph rm!!

CARTMAN
No you can't Kenny!

KENNY
Mph rm rmph!!

CARTMAN
Okay Kenny, I'll bet you a HUNDRED
DOLLARS you can't light a fart on fire!

KENNY
Mph mm!
Kenny pulls out a book of matches.
He strikes a match and holds it under his ass.
After a few seconds Kenny farts, and there is a little flame.
Suddenly, the flames catch and Kenny starts burning alive.

KENNY
MMMPMMMPH!!! MGMFEODFO!!!
Kenny runs around, and finally falls to the ground, still burning.

STAN
OH MY GOD!! YOU KILLED KENNY!!
KYLE
YOU BASTARD!!
Cartman looks shocked.

CARTMAN
Wow, I guess you CAN do that!

INT. HOSPITAL - LATER
DOCTORS and NURSES are pushing Kenny into the operating room
ER style.
Everything is quick and chaotic. Shouts fill the hallway.

NURSE
CBC chem kit STAT!!

DOCTOR GAUCHE

LOAD THAT I. V. WITH 70CCS OF SODIUM
PENTOTHAL!!
INT. OPERATING ROOM
It's mid-operation.

DOCTOR GAUCHE
Siphon the fluid off his brain!! Vacuum!
Another nurse hands him a sucker tube. He immediately shoves into Kenny's skull. It starts to slurp and burble.

DOCTOR GAUCHE
Try to untangle his trachea and esophagus!

NURSE
Right!
While Doctor Gauche wrestles with Kenny's lungs and torso, the nurse reaches into Kenny's mouth and pulls both his windpipe and esophagus out of his mouth, turning them inside out in the process.
Off to the side, Stan, Cartman and Kyle look on as the doctor and nurses tangle themselves in knots with Kenny's innards.

DOCTOR GAUCHE
No! THAT DOESN'T GO THERE!!

NURSE
Watch his liver!!!
Kenny's liver POPS out of his torso and slides across the floor.

ASSISTANT
I'll get it!!!

DOCTOR GAUCHE
We have precious little time left people!
We're going to lose him soon!!
Suddenly, there is a long, BEEEEEEEEEEEEEEEEEEEEEEEEEEP.

NURSE
Doctor, his heart's stopped!

DOCTOR GAUCHE
Crack him. Let's get it out of there!!!
Doctor Gauche lifts Kenny's heart out of his body.

DOCTOR GAUCHE
We need to zap this, quick!
And runs it to the microwave. He opens the door.

DOCTOR GAUCHE
Who's making a potato?

DOCTOR 2
My bad, sir. I missed lunch.

DOCTOR GAUCHE
Damn it! I am NOT going to lose this kid!!!!!!

INT. RECOVERY ROOM - LATER
Fade up from black. We're close on Kenny's face. His little eyes start to open.
Doctor Gauche leans over him Kenny. Stan and Kyle are there.

DOCTOR GAUCHE
Kenny. Kenny, can you hear me?
Kenny stirs.

KENNY
(Weakly)
Mph rmph rm...

DOCTOR GAUCHE
How are you feeling, son?

KENNY mph... . rmph... .

DOCTOR GAUCHE
Great... Son, I have some bad news. We accidentally replaced your heart with a baked
potato. You have about seven seconds to live.

KENNY
Mrm?!
Just then, Kenny's baked potato heart explodes, splattering gore all over the inside of the
recovery room and on the outside of Dr. Gauche, Stan and Kyle.

STAN
Oh my God! THEY killed Kenny!

KYLE

You bastards!!

DOCTOR GAUCHE
Damn it! It never gets any easier!
Anybody get the score of that Broncos game?

INT. HOSPITAL - WAITING ROOM
Kyle's mother is waiting with the rest of the parents.
The nurse walks up to Kenny's parents with a sad expression.

NURSE
I'm sorry...
Kenny's mother breaks down.

KENNY'S MOTHER
Oh my God, they killed Kenny!

KENNY'S DAD
You bastards!

KYLE'S MOTHER
I knew this would happen! Those bastard
Canadians have now killed a child! Can't people see the damage that film is doing?!

STAN'S MOTHER
He was killed doing something he saw in the movie. It was Terrance and Phillip...
THEY killed Kenny.

CARTMAN'S MOTHER
You bastards.

KYLE'S MOTHER
This is it! The time for action is NOW!!
(Singing)

Something must be done!
This is like a spreading rash!
They're pulling out our children's brains and filling them with trash!
Can't you see what this is leading to?
A world of smut and sex and poo!
I believe the good fight has begun!
Something must be done!
Everyone gathers around Kyle's mother.

32

STAN'S MOTHER
I agree!
(Singing)

Something must be done!
We must take action fast!
My child used to say 'please and thank you'
Now he says suck my ass!

CARTMAN'S MOTHER
And my boy was the sweetest boy the world had ever known! until those damn
Canadians brought that filth into our home!
I agree that there is now a battle to be won!
We can't just stand here singing!
Something must be done!

KENNY'S MOTHER
But what are we going to do against the media machine? It's so big and powerful!

KYLE'S MOTHER
Right! And we can use that same media machine to exploit OUR cause! We've got to let
the whole world know what the
Canadians did to your son!

PARENTS
Yeah!!

KYLE'S MOTHER
COME ON!
The parents all head out the door-

EXT. HOSPITAL - CONTINUOUS
The doors to the hospital swing open, and the parents march out into the street, singing in
unison as they go.

PARENTS
(Singing)

Something must be done!
Something's gotta give!
This world has become a bitch in which we have no desire to live!

Cars come screeching to a halt as the parents sing in the middle of the road. People start honking their horns in frustration.

KENNY'S MOTHER
My boy could have become a doctor
Or a lawyer rich and true
Instead he burned up like a piggy on a bar-b-que!

KYLE'S MOTHER
We will fight for children's rights in memory of your son!

PARENTS
We can't just stand here singing!
Something must be done!
Cars are now smashing into each other, and flying off the road to people's deaths, as the music number has taken over the busy intersection.

PARENTS
We've pushed and pushed it to the edge
And now the time has come!
Something's gotta change!
It's time to buy a gun!
We can't just stand here singing
No we can't just stand here singing
No we can't just stand here singing!
Something must be done!!!
A few more cars careen off and explode into flames as if ending the song with a borage of fireworks.

INT. OPERATING ROOM -
The boys gather around Kenny's lifeless body.

CARTMAN
(Dazed)
I bet him he couldn't do it... I bet him a hundred dollars!

KYLE
Come on, Cartman. It's not your fault.

CARTMAN
No, I know. I'm just fucking STOKED I don't have to pay him!

KYLE

Oh.

The boys walk out, leaving Kenny's corpse behind. We can still hear the boys voices as they exit.

KYLE (O. S.)
I can't believe he's dead.

CARTMAN (O. S.)
Yeah, I'm having total deja vu right now.
Like this has all happened before...
After they leave, PUSH IN to Kenny's dead body, which is left all alone on the operating table.
The camera continues to zoom in to Kenny's face...
ZOOM IN on Kenny's dead face. We pass into his thoughs...

FLASH!!
EXT. SPACE -
Kenny's body is floating through a great void. A PEACEFUL
SONG plays as he soars upwards to the heavens.
*note - except for Kenny's little construction paper body, this entire sequence should be done in 3D CGI.
Ahead of him, Kenny can see a great white light. It appears warm and inviting.
Now Kenny notices large beautiful breasts bobbing up and down in the heavens. He reaches out to touch them.
Kenny blissfully floats upward toward the bright light and bobbing breasts. The music crescendos as Kenny gets almost close enough to the light to touch it.
Just then, a huge, electronic sign pops up. 'Access Denied'.
Suddenly, Kenny goes spiraling downward. The song changes to a MINISTRY type number as Kenny's surroundings start to become darker and more twisted.
Kenny's hapless spirit enters a horrifying red tunnel, filled with flames and heat.

KENNY
Mph rmph rm!
Burning souls SCREAM and CRY all around Kenny, as his body plunges into what is now obviously the depths of hell.
Kenny passes images of Hitler, John Wayne Gacy, hunger and disease as he continues through the twisting tunnel.
He then passes images of Jimmy Stewart and Gandhi. All of whom are opportunely locked in hell for all eternity.

EXT. MOVIE THEATRE - DAY
The same ticket guy from before is at the ticket booth. The marquee still reads 'Terrance and Phillip' but a huge sticker has been placed over it that reads 'banned'.

The boys stand underneath the marquee looking baffled.

STAN
How can they do this?

KYLE
It isn't fair!

CARTMAN
Well, Terrance and Phillip are on Conan
O'Brian tonight, we could at least go watch that.
The boys hang their heads and walks away.
The ticket guy suddenly hears a bunch of commotion. He sees a mob of angry mothers, led by Kyle's mother.

KYLE'S MOTHER
THIS must be him, officer! This is the scum that sold R rated tickets to children!

TICKET GUY
What?! Jesus Christ, I didn't mean to!
Barbrady slaps handcuffs on the freaked out teen.

OFFICER BARBRADY
You can explain downtown!

TICKET GUY
(Getting dragged away)
Oh shit! Hey it's not MY fault! You should arrest those pervert Canadians!

KYLE'S MOTHER
Oh we will, Mr. Scumbag... We will...

EXT. CARTMAN'S HOUSE - NIGHT
Establishing.

INT. CARTMAN'S HOUSE - NIGHT
The boys are sitting on Cartman's couch watching TV.

ANGLE - TELEVISION - THE CONAN O'BRIAN SHOW
Conan comes back from a commercial break. Sitting next to him, is Ms. Brooke Shields.

CONAN O'BRIAN
Our next guests have the number one movie in the world right now, please welcome

Terrance and Phillip!
A few cheers as Terrance and Phillip walk out on stage. A few boos as well, and we see that the South Park mothers are in the audience holding 'Anti-Terrance and Phillip' signs. Terrance and Phillip walk out and sit next to Brooke Shields.

PHILLIP
Hello, Conan!

TERRANCE
Hello, Brooke Shields!

CONAN
It's nice to have you here in America.

PHILLIP
Yeah, well, you being a Canadian and all, we thought what the hell!

CONAN O'BRIAN
So guys... I understand you have a comedy routine worked out for us.

PHILLIP
We sure do, Conan. And here it is. Excuse me, Terrance.

TERRANCE
Yes, Phillip?
Phillip rips a fart that launches Terrance backwards and into the band. They both laugh wildly.

PHILLIP
Gotcha!
Terrance and Phillip laugh. Nobody in the audience laughs.

ANGLE - BOYS
They laugh merrily.

RESUME - THE CONAN O'BRIAN SHOW
TERRANCE
Good one, Phillip! Cheers.

PHILLIP
Cheers, Terrance!
Terrance extricates himself from the band. Conan is growing nervous. He looks out into the audience...

Kyle's mother is sitting there, looking angry. Conan makes eye contact with her, and then nods his head. Kyle's mother nods back.

CONAN O'BRIAN
(Nervous)
So, guys, I need to ask you a serious question...

PHILLIP
I just farted Terrance back into the stone age!
They both laugh hard.
Brooke Shields waits a beat, then belts out a fake laugh.

BROOKE SHIELDS
I farted once on the set of Blue Lagoon!

TERRANCE
Nobody cares, Brooke Shields!

CONAN O'BRIAN
Terrance and Phillip... Whose idea was it, to have a person lighting a fart on fire in your movie? Who is responsible for that?
Terrance and Phillip exhange glances.

TERRANCE
Phillip, I think our friend Conan has been working too hard.

CONAN O'BRIAN
Say it! It was YOUR idea to have someone light a fart on fire in your movie!

PHILLIP/TERRANCE
(Together)
It was our idea to have someone light a fart on fire in your movie.

ANGLE ON THE AUDIENCE
Kyle's mother is among them, listening to all this.

KYLE'S MOTHER
(Into her lapel)
That's it! Move, move, move!

ANGLE ON TERRANCE AND PHILLIP
A battalion of Army guys appear, seize Terrance and Phillip and arrest everyone in their group.

KYLE'S MOTHER

Terrance and Phillip, you are under arrest for working in America without the proper documents! WE GOT YOU!

ANGLE - BOYS

KYLE

Dude, what the hell is going on?

RESUME - THE CONAN O'BRIAN SHOW

TERRANCE

Phillip, we've been tricked and ambushed by The Conan O'Brian Show!!

PHILLIP

This little scrotum sucker willfully deceived us!
(Pointing to Conan)
You are a bad man!

TERRANCE

And you call yourself a Canadian!
(To Phillip)
I told you we should of done Leno!
Conan O'Brian turns away, ashamed.

KYLE'S MOTHER

Don't listen to them, Mr. O'Brian.
They're master manipulators. You did a good job.

TERRANCE

You loved our movie, Conan! We watched it together. You... You laughed!
Conan grabs his head.

CONAN O'BRIAN

What have I done?!!!
Conan grabs a gun and blows his head off, dousing Brooke
Shields with blood.

BROOKE SHIELDS

AGAHGAHGGH!!!! Mondays at eight

AAAGHGH!!!!

Terrance and Phillip laugh merrily. Kyle's mother cradles
Conan's lifeless body.

KYLE'S MOTHER
You see what your filth has caused?

TERRANCE
US?! This is your mess, outraged mother!!

INT. CARTMAN'S HOUSE - NIGHT
The boys are sitting on the couch in absolute shock.

STAN
Dude, our moms arrested Terrance and
Phillip!

KYLE
Our moms suck!

CARTMAN
This could mean... No more Terrance and
Phillip - EVER!

EXT. UNITED NATIONS - DAY
Establishing shot.

INT. UNITED NATIONS - GENERAL ASSEMBLY ROOM
Lots of foreigners with their silly foreign outfits sit at their stupid microphones with their ridiculous translation headsets -- in the general assembly hall. The Canadian Ambassador stands before them.

CANADIAN AMBASSADOR
As The Canadian Ambassador, I hereby condemn the actions taken by America in apprehending Terrance and Phillip!
A MURMUR goes through the crowd.

CANADIAN AMBASSADOR
We demand their release IMMEDIATELY!! As you can see from this graph, the entire economy of Canada relies on Terrance and
Phillip! Without them we are doomed to recession!
The United Nations head bangs his gavel.
Now Kyle's mother stands up. She is with a group of mothers all wearing M. A. C T-shirts.

KYLE'S MOTHER

If I may?
Everyone looks at Kyle's mother.

KYLE'S MOTHER
As president and founder of M. A. C. , I would like to state-

UNITED NATIONS HEAD
Excuse me, M. A. C. ?

KYLE'S MOTHER
Yes, Mothers Against Canada.

UNITED NATIONS HEAD
Kay.

KYLE'S MOTHER
I would like to state that Canada must learn to stop infiltrating our country with its graphic art!
Cheers from the Americans.

CANADIAN AMBASSADOR
Last time I checked America was a free country!

KYLE'S MOTHER
Look at this!
Kyle's mother pulls Kenny's mother up by the head.

KYLE'S MOTHER
This woman's child was KILLED by your country's humor! Look how upset she is!
Kenny's mom looks fine.

CANADIAN AMBASSADOR
We will continue to sell Terrance and
Phillip videos to anyone retarded enough to buy it!!

KYLE'S MOTHER
Then you leave me no choice... I call for an EMBARGO on ALL Canadian Imports!!!
More cheers from the Americans. The Canadians look worried.

INT. SUPERMARKET - DAY
The boys are in the check out line at Bob's supermarket.

CARTMAN

What the hell do you mean I can't get
Cheesy Poofs?!

BOB
Sorry, kid. Cheesy Poofs are a Canadian export. We can't carry them any more.

KYLE
Who the hell made up that law?!

CARTMAN
You can't do this!! Have you ever HAD
Cheesy Poofs? They're a taste sensation with a delightful cheddar crunch.

BOB
There's nothing I can do. I can still sell you Cheese-o's.

CARTMAN
FUCK Cheese-os and FUCK you!
Cartman storms out. The boys follow him.

INT. CARTMAN'S HOUSE - DAY
The boys walk into Cartman's house. Cartman slams the door behind him. The boys all walk toward the living room.

CARTMAN
Come on, you guys... We have to THINK!

STAN
About what?

CARTMAN
About Cheesy Poofs, dumbass! This whole thing has gone too far!

KYLE
I don't really think you need Cheesy-
Poofs, tubby-
But the boys come to an abrupt halt when they reach the living room and see that all four mothers are waiting for them, silently.
Everyone just sits there for a second. The lighting on Kyle's mother's face looks almost evil.

KYLE'S MOTHER
Boys, we have to have a difficult discussion.

KYLE
We already know what you did. We saw it on television.

STAN
Yeah, how come you arrested Terrance and
Phillip?

STAN'S MOTHER
Stanly, you're too young to understand what's good for you. That's why we mothers have
taken charge.

KYLE
But they fucking didn't do anything wrong!

CARTMAN
Yeah! And what rim job expert went and outlawed Cheesy Poofs!?
The mothers all gasp in horror.

KYLE'S MOTHER
What was that word, young man!?

CARTMAN'S MOTHER
Oh, he said rim job. It's when someone licks your ass for-

KYLE'S MOTHER
I know what it is!

CARTMAN
(To his mother)
Lick someone's ass?!

KYLE'S MOTHER
The Terrance and Phillip movie has obviously done irreparable damage to their brains.
We have to put them in rehab right away.

KYLE
What's that?

KYLE'S MOTHER
You boys need help. There are rehab centers that specialize in treating people with
chronic addictions to bad language.

STAN'S MOTHER
There are?
Kyle's mother thinks for a second.

KYLE'S MOTHER
Well no, I guess not... But we will establish the first of its kind right here in South Park. All the children in town will have to attend and receive treatment from the school counselor Mr.
Mackey! Ooh I just love when I get these sorts of ideas!

CARTMAN
Why? So you can fuck up our life some more?

CARTMAN'S MOTHER
Eric! Don't talk to Ms. Brovlofski that way!

CARTMAN
But mom! I'm not fucking addicted to fucking bad language! I don't have a fucking problem!

INT. HELL - DAY
Kenny walks through the black void of hell. A trippy, single shaft of light seems to follow him wherever he goes.

KENNY
Mphrmo?
No answer... No nothing...
Kenny continues on, flames shoot up randomly from the ground scaring the shit out of him.

KENNY
MPHR!! MMLY MMT!
Suddenly, Kenny hears a CLAWING NOISE. It gets louder and louder. Kenny starts to run faster and faster. Now the clawing is RIGHT BEHIND HIM! Kenny spins around. He is face to face with SATAN!
Satan looks down at Kenny and shoots flames out his nose.
Kenny's eyes bulge open.

KENNY
MMMMMPHPHPHPHP!!!!!
SATAN
Fallen one... We have such sights to show you!

Kenny shakes. Satan turns to a whispy form and flashes across the room like a serpent, in a millisecond he is right up in
Kenny's face.

SATAN
I am Satan. I am your God, now.

KENNY
MPH RM!!!
Kenny tries to run away, but Satan again changes form, flies across the room and cuts Kenny off.

SATAN
Come with me. I will show you what delightful pain awaits.
Two black DEMONS grab Kenny by the arms and start to lead him away.

KENNY
MMMMMPHPHP!!!!
Just then, SADDAM HUSSEIN show up next to Satan.

SADDAM HUSSEIN
Oh, a new recruit, huh? Welcome to hell, kid! Relax! Take a load off!!

SATAN
You remember... Saddam Hussein, don't you?!
Kenny's eyes grow wide.

KENNY
MMMPPH!!!
EXT. REHAB CENTER - DAY
Establishing shot of the small Betty Fordesque building.

INT. REHAB CENTER - SOUTH PARK'S BETTY FORD CENTER
The kids are sitting in chairs in a circle. There are anti- drug signs on the walls: "Crack is Whack"; "Get High on
Pottery"; and, "I Go From Zero to Bitch in . 9 Seconds. " MR.
MACKEY, the wiry school counselor, leads the group. There's a pottery wheel and lots of craft tables behind them.

MR. MACKEY
Mkay, it's come to my attention, that you boys have a potty-mouth problem, mkay.
Now the sooner you recognize your problem, mkay, the sooner we can get you back to your third grade homeroom where you belong.

KYLE
But they're just words, Mr. Mackey. Our parents are over-reacting.

BEBE
Yeah, Wendy's here, and she doesn't even like Terrance and Phillip!
Wendy looks bored. Stan tries to smile at her, but she doesn't even acknowledge him.
Meanwhile, Cartman is violently shaking in his seat.

CARTMAN
Ugh... You guys, seriously... I'm having
Cheesy Poof withdrawal...

MR. MACKEY
Mkay, kids from all over the State have been brought here, because you all share the
same problem. Uh, young man... Let's start with you.
He points at Gregory. The little British bastard from the lake.

GREGORY
My name is Gregory... And I have a potty mouth.
Wendy looks at Gregory. Stan notices this.

CARTMAN
You've got a stupid accent too.

MR. MACKEY
Eric, that is not appropriate.

CARTMAN
What? Fuck French people. Fuck 'em in the ear.

MR. MACKEY
Mkay, you see, children. This is exactly what I'm talking about. We have to change the
way you think.

GREGORY
How are you gonna do that?
Mr. Mackey crosses to a piano. He plays chords while speaking the following lines.

MR. MACKEY
There are times when you get suckered in, by drugs and alcohol and sex with wom-en.
But it's when you do these things too much
(Singing)

That you've got to clear your head and get back in touch...
Mr. Mackey plays the piano and sings:

MR. MACKEY
You can do it, it's all up to you, mkay?
With a method, there's nothing you can't do, mkay?
You don't have to spend your life addicted to crack
Homeless on the streets giving hand- jobs for cash as long as you follow this simple plan
I'm fully convinced that it's, easy, mkay...
The kids are extremely disinterested. Mackey walks over to a chalkboard.

MR. MACKEY
Step one: Think about fun. Think about all that you'll miss addicted to this
Step two: Think it all through.
Think how's this gonna change my life, what am I gonna miss?
Step three: Go and hug a tree, Hug anything that gets in your way!
And step four: Just don't do it anymore - it's easy, Mkay!
Mackey gets the children in a circle all holding hands.

MR. MACKEY
Come on, kids! Sing along!

KIDS
(Extremely half-assed)

You can do it, it's all up to you mkay?
With a method, there's nothing you can't do, mkay?
We don't have to spend our lives addicted to crack
Homeless on the streets giving hand- jobs for cash

MR. MACKEY
As long as you follow my simple plan
I'm fully convinced that it's, easy, mkay...
Everyone starts dancing in a circle.

KIDS
Step one: Think about fun. Think about all that you'll miss addicted to this Step two: Think it all through. Think how's this gonna change my life, what am I gonna miss?
Step three: Go and hug a tree, Hug anything that gets in your way!
And step four: Just don't do it anymore - it's easy, Mkay!

MR. MACKEY
It's easy, Mkay?!
Everyone falls down laughing.

INT. REHAB CENTER - LOUNGE
Kyle's mom and the other moms watch the kids and Mr. Mackey rolling around on the floor laughing on a security monitor.

KYLE'S MOTHER
What the hell do they think this is?!
Summer camp?!

INT. REHAB CENTER - SOUTH PARK'S BETTY FORD CENTER
Just then, Kyle's mother walks in with a scowling look, interupting the kids and Mr. Mackey who are still laughing merrily. The other mothers are behind her.

KYLE'S MOTHER
Mr. Mackey, what is going on?!
Mr. Mackey stands up, looking scared.

MR. MACKEY
Uh, we're just, starting our program...

KYLE'S MOTHER
This is NOT a place for fun and games!
This is rehabilitation! Now GET TO IT!!
We at MAC have a trial to go to!
The mothers walk away.

MR. MACKEY
Mkay.

CARTMAN
God Damn it your mom is a bitch, Kyle.
Kyle hangs his head.

EXT. SUPREME COURT - DAY
A news reporter stands in front of the Supreme Court. All around him are protestors, with signs that say CANADA NO! and
CAN'TADA! Still others hold signs with Kenny on them.

NEWS REPORTER

Tom I'm standing in front of the U. S.

Supreme Court where the most important trial of the - day - is happening.

Thousands of people have shown up from all over the country to show their outrage and disgust at Canada. Joining me now is Mrs. McKormick, mother of the poor little boy who was killed by the

Canadians.

Kenny's mother steps into frame. She is wearing a shirt with

Kenny's picture on it. Written on the T-shirt is 'Have you seen my son? No, you haven't. He's dead. '

NEWS REPORTER

Mrs. McKormick, you must really hate the
Canadians.

KENNY'S MOTHER

Yes, yes I do, Tom.

NEWS REPORTER

Did you ever think you would see the day when thousands of people were wearing your son Kenny on T-shirts?

KENNY'S MOTHER

No I didn't. But if any of you would like one they're 14. 95. Available in blue or white.

The reporter thinks for a second, and then turns back to the camera.

NEWS REPORTER

Well, we can only imagine the intense, vehement trial that is going on inside.

INT. SUPREME COURT - DAY

Terrance and Phillip are on the stand.

JOHNNY COCHRAN

Terrance and Phillip... You knowingly, with malice of forethought were trying to destroy American culture, yes or no?

Terrance rips a fart.

JOHNNY COCHRAN
YES OR NO!
INT. REHAB CENTER - SOUTH PARK'S BETTY FORD CENTER

The kids are all in the main room, sitting on a couch, huddled around a television.

They laugh merrily.

STAN

Shh! Mr. Mackey's gonna hear us!

INT. SUPREME COURT - DAY
TERRANCE
The Americans are just showing their TRUE
COLORS as smelly bastards.

PHILLIP
Fight the power!

TERRANCE
The young boy that died lit himself on fire. It was unfortunate, but how can they blame
US?

PHILLIP
Don't believe the hype!!
Terrance and Phillip laugh merrily.

INT. REHAB CENTER - SOUTH PARK'S BETTY FORD CENTER
The kids all shout agreement.

KIDS
(Adlib)
Yeah! WooHoo!

BACK TO COURTHOUSE
Terrance and Phillip laugh merrily.

TERRANCE
You cannot oppress us! We will continue to pursue our art. We know there are
Americans out there who will help us!
Kyle's mother now stands up from the prosecutor's table.

KYLE'S MOTHER
Your 'ART' is shallow and immature! We
Americans do NOT allow that for our children!!

PHILLIP
Please. You teach your children that
America is the land of the free. But it's all bullshit. You're one of the most conservative
countries in the world!

INT. REHAB CENTER - SOUTH PARK'S BETTY FORD CENTER

The children all listen, wide-eyed.

INT. SUPREME COURT - DAY
TERRANCE
The problem is you don't allow your children to think for themselves. You try to raise them in a protective bubble, and then when they finally get old enough, they realize they've been lied to, and they resent you for it.

PHILLIP
Yeah, God, no wonder your country is so fucked up.

KYLE'S MOTHER
THAT IS ENOUGH!!
TERRANCE
WAKE UP AMERICA! YOUR government censors
YOU from the world.

KYLE'S MOTHER
NO THEY DON'T!
PHILLIP
YES THEY DO! AND I'LL PROVE IT TO YOU! IN
MARCH OF LAST YEAR, THE AMERICAN
GOVERNMENT-
BOOOOOOOOOOOOOOOOOOOOOOOOOOOOOOOOOOOP.
Suddenly, the screen goes blank. A sign that says 'PLEASE
STAND BY' comes on.

INT. REHAB CENTER - SOUTH PARK'S BETTY FORD CENTER
The kids all watch, wide-eyed.

KYLE
What happened?

WENDY
The station CONVENIENTLY went blank.

INT. CANADIAN PRESS CONFERENCE - DAY
The Canadian Prime Minister stands directly in front of camera, looking right at us.

CANADIAN PRIME MINISTER
ATTENTION AMERICA!! You have taken our national treasure Terrance and Phillip. We, in turn, have taken yours... The
Smothers Brothers!

The Canadian Prime Minister steps out of the way, revealing the Smothers Brothers tied up in chairs behind him.

CANADIAN PRIME MINISTER
I'll let you catch your breath... Now, release Terrance and Phillip, or else we will EXECUTE your beloved Smothers
Brothers!!

TOMMY SMOTHERS
Please listen to them!!

DICK SMOTHERS
They're not fucking around!!

CANADIAN PRIME MINISTER
We're not fucking around. This is not aboot deals. This aboot dignity. This is aboot freedom... This is aboot respect.
RETURN Terrance and Phillip NOW!!!
Another Canadian leans in and whispers in the Prime
Minister's ear.

CANADIAN PRIME MINISTER
Oh yeah... AND FUCK YOU, AMERICA!
He raises his middle finger, but it's all blurred and digitized.

INT. REHAB CENTER - SOUTH PARK'S BETTY FORD CENTER
MR. MACKEY
Okay kids, for today's rehabilitation activity, we're going to watch the
Terrance and Phillip movie.

STAN
What?!

KYLE
Sweet!

MR. MACKEY
Now, this is an EDITED version of the movie, which was put out by the MPAA.
That's the Motion Picture Association of
America.

WENDY
Isn't that censorship?

MR. MACKEY
No the MPAA is NOT a censorship group.

WENDY
Why not?

MR. MACKEY
Uh... Because they say so... Mkay. Now I want you to watch this movie, with all the immature profanity taken out, and notice how much better a movie it becomes...
Mackey puts the tape in and hits play.
The TITLES come up 'Terrance and Phillip Asses of Fire'
Except that 'Asses' has been blurred out, and replaced with
'bunz'.

KIDS
HOORAY!!!
The movie begins. Phillip walks in. But it isn't Phillip's voice, somebody has dubbed him over.

DUBBED PHILLIP
Hey Terrance. I feel like I'm going to pass gas near your head.

DUBBED TERRANCE
I would rather you didn't, Phillip.

DUBBED PHILLIP
Oh? Is that so?
Phillip farts on Terrance.

TERRANCE
Oh, you are such a maroon!

PHILLIP
You would know, dummy.
The boys look confused.

TERRANCE
You are pigeon-like in your intelligence.
The pseudo-Terrance and Phillip laugh. Terrance throws a match on Phillip and Phillip burns to death.
A TITLE comes up - THE END.
And the credits roll.

CARTMAN
WHAT THE HELL WAS THAT?!
KYLE
Dude, they cut out 92 minutes!
The lights in the theater come up.

MR. MACKEY
So you see, the point and the theme of the film is kept intact. And of course, the MPAA didn't cut out any of the graphic violence. What did you think?

CARTMAN
Oh man, I'm gonna need a cherry pie to get the taste of ass out of my mouth from that piece of shit movie.

MR. MACKEY
Eric, you're not watching your mouth!

CARTMAN
You get me Cheesy Poofs with the delightful cheddar crunch, and I'll watch my fucking mouth!

MR. MACKEY
Eric!!!! You need to be rehabilitated.
Help me to help you!

CARTMAN
Help yourself prickfuck!

MR. MACKEY
I am not a prickfuck, mkay? You little asshole!
Mackey slaps his hand over his mouth and looks around, scared.

CARTMAN
Ha, ha, you stupid asshole prickfuck.

INT. REHAB CENTER - SEPARATE ROOM
Mr. Mackey is in a private office with the members of M. A. C.

KYLE'S MOTHER
How is the children's progress?

MR. MACKEY

Very encouraging. Most of the children have been weened from their naughty mouths.

KYLE'S MOTHER
What do you mean MOST, why not ALL?

MR. MACKEY
(Nervous)
Well, some of the children just don't respond to 12 step programs.

KYLE'S MOTHER
Then we'll have to resort to plan B and call the v-chip organization.
Dramatic MUSIC STING. Mackey looks afraid.

MR. MACKEY
Mrs. Brovlofski, the V-chip hasn't been fully tested yet, it could be dangerous.

KYLE'S MOTHER
(Evil)
I don't care if it's dangerous! Desperate times call for desperate measures, Mr.
Mackey. Perhaps I need to remind you of your situation.

MR. MACKEY
(Nervous)
Alright, I'll make the call...

INT. REHAB CENTER - SOUTH PARK'S BETTY FORD CENTER
The kids are again glued to the TV watching the trial of
Terrance and Phillip.

INT. SUPREME COURT - DAY
Back in the courthouse, the jury walks in and sits down.

JUDGE
Madam foreman, have you reached a verdict?

FOREMAN
We have, your honor.

JUDGE
How find you, the jury?

FOREMAN
We the jury, find the defendants...

Terrance and Phillip... GUILTY of being complete bastards.
The crowd goes wild. The mothers of M. A. C. stand and cheer.

INT. REHAB CENTER - SOUTH PARK'S BETTY FORD CENTER
The kids sit in shock.

KYLE
Oh no!

INT. COURTROOM - DAY
TERRANCE
Oh oh, Phillip. You know what this means?

PHILLIP
We'll be farting bread and water for a few years.
The judge bangs her gavel.

JUDGE
Terrance and Phillip, for crimes against the great nation of America you are hereby
sentenced to DEATH.

HUGE MUSIC STING.
TERRANCE
DEATH?! You gotta be shittin' me!

PHILLIP
Aghgh!
Phillip passes out.

INT. REHAB CENTER - SOUTH PARK'S BETTY FORD CENTER
The kids can't believe what they're seeing. Everyone is silent. Finally, Kyle perks up.

KYLE
Dude, let's help Terrance and Phillip!!

STAN
How do we do that?
Kyle thinks for a moment.

WENDY
You raise awareness by distributing buttons, stickers and leaflets.

CARTMAN

That'd be sweet! We could try to bring back Cheesy Poofs!

KYLE
Yeah, let's make Free Terrance and
Phillip buttons!

WENDY
You guys don't even care. All you care about is seeing Terrance and Phillip fart on each other more.
The boys sit there and blink.

STAN
Yeah!

WENDY
This is about freedom of speech, Stan, about censorship.
The handsome English kid, Gregory chimes in.

GREGORY
Yes, what's next? Barcodes on our forearms? This country is the most fascist of all.
Wendy looks at Gregory deeply. Gregory smiles at her.

STAN
What the hell are you talking about, kid?

WENDY
You don't get it Stan... You just don't get it.
Wendy walks away.

STAN
What? What don't I get?
(To Kyle)
What don't I get?

KYLE
I don't know, dude.

STAN
That British dickhole is what's taking
Wendy away from me!

KYLE
I thought she wasn't your girlfriend, dude.

STAN
She's Not! But if she WAS it would be
THAT little asshole who's fucking it up for me!

INT. REHAB CENTER - SOUTH PARK'S BETTY FORD CENTER
The kids are all sitting in rows, wearing very crude 'Free
Terrance and Phillip' buttons.

MR. MACKEY
Mkay, children, you've all made terrific progress, and are hereby done with the eight step program.
The kids all AD LIB relief.

CARTMAN
Thank God, that sucked ass.

MR. MACKEY
Uh, except for you Eric. I'm afraid you need to work more on not saying the F word and the N word.

CARTMAN
The N word?

MR. MACKEY
(Reading)
Norwegian Ass Raper.

CARTMAN
Oh yeah.

MR. MACKEY
The rest of you are graduated. You can go home today.
The kids cheer.

CARTMAN
I don't graduate?! WHAT THE FUCK IS

THIS?! THIS IS BULLSHIT?!
Just then, Mackey notices the little buttons on everybody's shirts.

MR. MACKEY
Free Terrance and Phillip? Oh no... Mkay.

KYLE
(Proudly)
We're protesting!

STAN
Yeah!

MR. MACKEY
Well, boys, it might interest you to know that your FRIENDS the Canadians have just bombed the U. S.

STAN
They did?!

MR. MACKEY
Yes, at six this morning they bombed the heck out of Cleveland.

KYLE
Oh. That doesn't count.

WENDY
They only bombed Cleveland because we're going to Execute two of their citizens!!

MR. MACKEY
Wendy, Mkay, if you want to start getting political, I'll throw your skinny little butt right back into rehab. Mkay?

CARTMAN
HOW THE FUCK CAN YOU NOT GRADUATE ME?!
DOES THAT MEAN I HAVE TO STAY HERE?!
MR. MACKEY
No, Eric... I'm afraid it's phase two for you...
Dramatic MUSIC sting.

INT. HELL - DAY
Kenny is chained up in a torture chamber in Hell. Demons and ghouls surround him.

SATAN
Prepare thyself for unending pain!
Unparalleled misery!!
Kenny starts to cry.
Saddam Hussein comes out from behind Satan holding a martini.

59

SADDAM HUSSEIN
Hey, relax Satan. Don't get all worked up. You're gonna give yourself an ulcer again.

KENNY
Mrph mprph!!

SADDAM HUSSEIN
What? What do you mean you don't belong here? Relax guy, hell is for children.

KENNY
Mrph mprhm mm rmph!

SADDAM HUSSEIN
A deal? You wanna make a deal with the devil. Well sure, deals are mounds o' fun.

SATAN
(To Saddam)
Saddam, would you let me do my job please!

SADDAM HUSSEIN
Hey relax, guy. Let's see what the kid wants.

KENNY
Mph rmph rm rmph rmph rm!

SADDAM HUSSEIN
Oh, you want out of hell, huh?

SATAN
Well of COURSE he wants out of hell! The whole POINT of hell is that you don't WANT to be here!

SADDAM HUSSEIN
Okay, kid, I have a deal for you! If you want out of hell, all you have to do is collect 10 proofs of purchases from
'Snacky Smores. ' They're rich, chocolatey and really hit the spot. Bring me ten proofs of purchases and we'll grant you ANY WISH YOU WANT.

KENNY
Mrph?

SADDAM HUSSEIN

I wouldn't bullshit you kid! Snacky
Smores are now available in stores everywhere! No biggie!
Saddam walks over to Kenny and releases his chains.

SADDAM HUSSEIN
(To Kenny)
Well what are you waiting for pal?! Get to it!
Kenny runs out and away.

SADDAM HUSSEIN
HA HA HAHA!! What a dumbass!!
Saddam walks over and joins Satan on the couch.

SATAN
I don't see why you have to belittle me in front of people like that.

SADDAM HUSSEIN
Hey, relax guy. It's just a cruel joke.
Rich, chocolatey Snacky Smores are only available up on Earth. He'll never get
'em, see?

SATAN
Sometimes I just think you don't have any respect for me.

SADDAM HUSSEIN
Hey, come here, guy.
Saddam pulls Satan around and plants a big wet kiss on him.

SADDAM HUSSEIN
Who's my cream puff?

SATAN
I am.

INT. PTA MEETING - DAY
A large crowd of parents has gathered for a PTA meeting.
Kenny's mother is at a table selling dead Kenny t-shirts. She has a shitload of money all
around her. Another MOTHER walks up, hands Kenny's mom money, and gets a shirt.

MOTHER
Is that a new pearl bracelet, Mrs.
McKormick?

KENNY'S MOTHER
Why yes. Yes it is.
Meanwhile, Kyle's mother is on the stand.

KYLE'S MOTHER
As our next official order of business here at M. A. C. , we will test the new V- chip. As most of you know, the V-chip was created to lock children out of watching certain shows on television. And now the
N. I. H. has created a new, exciting product that they can tell us all about.
Here is the Surgeon General, Dr.
Pangloss.
DOCTOR PANGLOSS, a lab technician in white takes the podium.

DOCTOR PANGLOSS
Thank you, parents.
One person claps. Pangloss hits a button and a slide projector starts showing pictures of the device.

DOCTOR PANGLOSS
The machinery of the new 'V-chip' is very simple, and similar to that of the V- chip. The chip is placed just under the subject's skin, where it emits a small but painful shock of electricity whenever an obscenity is uttered.
The parents are fascinated.

STAN'S FATHER
Now wait a minute, are you telling us that this chip somehow KNOWS if the kid is swearing?

DOCTOR PANGLOSS
It's just like a lie detector. Certain things happen in you when you swear just like when you lie, the chip picks up on this and gives the subject a shock.
The parents AD LIB 'Ooohs' and 'Ahhhhs'

DOCTOR PANGLOSS
We are very excited to see the results of this test.
(Calling)
Patient 453, would you step out here, please?
Cartman steps out wearing a hospital gown.

DOCTOR PANGLOSS
Patient 453 here has been fitted with the new v-chip...

CARTMAN

My head hurts.

DOCTOR PANGLOSS
Don't worry about that. Now, I want you to say 'Doggy. '

CARTMAN
Doggy.

DOCTOR PANGLOSS
Notice that nothing happens.
(To Cartman)
Now say 'Montana. '

CARTMAN
Montana.

DOCTOR PANGLOSS
Good. Now 'Pillow'.

CARTMAN
Pillow.

DOCTOR PANGLOSS
Alright, now I want you to say
'horsefucker. '
Cartman looks offstage to his mother.

CARTMAN'S MOTHER
Go ahead, it's alright, Eric.
Cartman smiles.

CARTMAN
Horsefuck-

BZZZZZAAAAT!!!!
CARTMAN
AGAAHGAHGAH!!!!!
Cartman falls to the floor in pain. All the parents ooh and ahh and applaud.

CARTMAN
OW!! That HURT GOD DAMMI-

BAZAAATTT!!

CARTMAN
OW!! YOU CAN'T DO THIS TO ME!! THIS ISN'T
FAIR!!! YOU SONS A BITCHE--
BAZAAATTT!!

DOCTOR PANGLOSS
Success!! Our device works perfectly! We will begin mass production immediately!

KYLE'S MOTHER
And so we have succesfully removed the
Canadian smut from all of our children's brains.
We have made changes at school to ensure that our kids are NEVER AGAIN exposed to smut!!!!!!! It's OVER!
The crowd goes wild.

EXT. SCHOOL - DAY
School is now Naziesque. A military drum echoes in the distance.

INT. CLASSROOM - SOUTH PARK ELEMENTARY - DAY
Stan and Kyle are sitting in their desks, waiting for school to begin.
Wendy walks by on her way to her desk.

STAN
Hi Wendy.

WENDY
(Not even looking)
Hi Stan.
Wendy walks on by.

KYLE
Wow, dude. Wendy could really give a rats ass about you.

STAN
(Eyes still on Wendy)
I bet she would if my name was GREGORY!!

KYLE
Good thing she was never your girlfriend... Dude, here comes Cartman.
Cartman walks in and gingerly sits down.

KYLE
Hey, Cartman, did they put that V-chip in your head or your ass?

64

STAN
What's the difference?
Stan and Kyle laugh.

CARTMAN
Very funny dickhead-
BZZAAT! The v-chip shocks Cartman.

CARTMAN
OW! FUCK-
BZZZAAAT!!
CARTMAN
AY!
Cartman is thrown to the floor in a shivering heap.

KYLE
Whoa! What the hell was that?!

STAN
Dude! It's the V-chip! It shocks him ever time he cusses!
Stan and Kyle look at each other. Kyle smiles.

KYLE
Hey Cartman.

CARTMAN
What?

KYLE
You know, me and Stan were just talking about what a fat fucking hunk o' fat fuck you are.

CARTMAN
Oh yeah?! Well you're a monkey-shit-

BZAAAT!
CARTMAN
SHIT-
BZZZAAAT!!
CARTMAN
FUCK-
BZZAAAT!! The cycle continues as Stan and Kyle laugh merrily watching Cartman flopping around on the floor.

KYLE
This is sweet!!

STAN
Totally!
Garrison stands before his class.

MR. GARRISON
Okay, children, let's try a few new math problems. What is five times two?
The kids all just sit there.

MR. GARRISON
Come on, children, do be shy, just give it your best shot.
Clyde raises his hand.

MR. GARRISON
Yes, Clyde?

CLYDE
Twelve?

MR. GARRISON
Okay, now let's try to get an answer from somebody who's not a complete retard.
Anyone? Come on don't be shy...
Just then, the door bursts open and in walks a couple of Nazi looking American soldiers.
They walk over to the children and start pulling off their
'Free Terrance and Phillip' pins.

STAN
Hey, what are you doing?

SOLDIER
You can't wear these in school. It's against school policy, thank you.
Another solider rips off Kyle's pin and replaces it with a yellow star.

KYLE
What's that for?

SOLDIER 2
You get a star for doing well in school.
Just as quickly, the soldiers make their way out the door.

WENDY
NAZIS!!
STAN
What's the matter, Wendy?

WENDY
Nothing, Stan. You wouldn't understand.

STAN
(To Kyle)
God damn it, why does she keep saying that?

INT. CAFETERIA - DAY
The boys are in line. Nazi-ish soldiers usher them through.

STAN
I'm so sick of these soldiers.

KYLE
Yeah, they suck.

CARTMAN
I know. Always saying, do this, do that.
They think they're so cooool.
(To the soldier)
Acht lieben kraft auct shpiler!

(BZZZT)
OW!!!
The soldier glares at him. The boys walk into the kitchen, where they are greeted by their big, happy, black school

CHEF!
CHEF
Hello there, children!!

STAN
Hey, Chef.

CHEF
How would like some Salisbury Steak with buttered noodles?

KYLE

We can't, we're on a hunger strike.

CHEF
A hunger strike? For what?

STAN
To free Terrance and Phillip.

CARTMAN
But you guys... It's Salisbury steak.

STAN
Chef, do you know anything about women?

CHEF
Ha! Is the Pope Catholic?

KYLE
I don't know.

CHEF
Children, I know ALL there is to know about women.

STAN
What's the secret to making a woman happy?

CHEF
(Dishing out food)
Oh that's easy, you just gotta find the clitoris.

STAN
Huh?
Suddenly, Chef realizes who he's talking to.

CHEF
Oops, I guess you haven't got that far in your anatomy class, huh?

STAN
No, what does that mean, find the clitoris?

CARTMAN
Is that like finding Jesus or something?
Now Chef starts to panic.

CHEF
Uh... Nothing. Forget I said anything.
Now move along, children! You're holding up the line!
Just then, the P. A. blares out an announcement.

PRINCIPAL VICTORIA (O. S.)
ATTENTION ALL SOUTH PARK ELEMENTARY
STUDENTS AND STAFF! REPORT TO THE
GYMNASIUM IMMEDIATELY FOR A SPECIAL
ANNOUNCEMENT!!
STAN
Woa, I wonder what's going on, dude.

INT. GYMNASIUM - DAY
All the elementary students are gathered in front of a large television monitor.
Mr. Garrison and his class walk in and look confused.
The boys walk up to Chef.

PRINCIPAL VICTORIA
Please take your seats, everyone!!!!
They all go to their seats.

KYLE
What's going on, Chef?

CHEF
Something big, children.
The television goes from that Emergency broadcast signal to a scene of a news anchor
sitting at his desk.

NEWS ANCHOR
(Very serious)
This is a State of Emergency. We go now to the White House for a VERY IMPORTANT
ANNOUNCEMENT from the President of the
United States.

INT. OVAL OFFICE - DAY
The President is sitting in a chair by the fireplace.

PRESIDENT CLINTON
Ladies and gentlemen... At five a. m. today, a day which will live in infamy... sort of...
the U. S. has declared war on

Canada.

ANGLE - KIDS
They all stare in silence. Mr. Garrison takes a deep breath.

CHEF
Oh, no...

MR. MACKEY
I don't believe it.

CARTMAN
Holy crap-

(BZZZT!)
OW!! Hey crap isn't a swear word, what the fuck?!

(ZZZZZZTTT)
AGAGAGH!!!
PRESIDENT CLINTON
All Canadians are to leave the country immediately, or be subject to military camps. All Canadian products are to be thrown out.

PRINCIPAL VICTORIA
How can they do this?

MR. GARRISON
I never thought there would be war again in my lifetime...

INT. WHITE HOUSE - DAY
PRESIDENT CLINTON
Do not be afraid of this war. Instead embrace it. We have God on our side. And besides, they're just Canadians, what the hell are they gonna do?

INT. GYMNASIUM - DAY
Everyone watches the television in stunned silence.

STAN
Chef, what does it mean that we're at war?

CHEF
It's... It's not good children.

PRINCIPAL VICTORIA
What do we do? Do we go on as normal or... ?

MR. GARRISON
I don't know Principal Victoria... I don't know...

PRESIDENT
And now, I would like to bring up the woman who led, and is still leading the way in this glorious stand-

KYLE
(Pointing to TV)

HOLY SHIT DUDE!!
Kyle's mom appears on the TV dressed in military garb.

PRESIDENT
Mrs. Sheila Brovlofski.

CHEF
Isn't that your mother, Kyle?
Kyle can't believe it.
On the television, Kyle's mother walks up to the podium. She is dressed to the hilt. She hugs the President and the first lady and then takes a deep breath.

KYLE'S MOTHER
My fellow Americans. I have led this fight in the War against profanity. I have founded Mothers Against Canada. Our neighbor to the north has abused us for the last time.

PRESIDENT
As Commander in chief, I have ordered our
Army to set up defensive positions along the US-Canada border in anticipation of an attack.

KYLE'S MOTHER
What about air strikes?

PRESIDENT
Huh?

KYLE'S MOTHER
We have to have air strikes on their military and entertainment centers. It's the only way to ensure that their smut can't reach American soil!

PRESIDENT
Oh, uh... I don't know if air strikes are necessary.

KYLE'S MOTHER
Not necessary?! Mr. President, may I remind you that our country's heart and soul are at stake, and our children's minds are the battlefield!
The bastard Canadians want to fight us because we won't tolerate their potty mouths. Well, if it is war they want...

THEN WAR THEY SHALL HAVE!!!
A huge eruption of cheers from the crowd in front of Kyle's mother. She is obviously floored by it. She can't help but smile. She actually holds her head up higher, and then raises her arms up in two peace signs, as the cheers get louder.
The president forces a smile and actually applauds with the rest of the crowd.
Back in the gymnasium, Kyle looks thoroughly embarrassed.

CHEF
Damn, your mom's a bitch, Kyle.

CARTMAN
Amen to that.

INT. HELL - DAY
Kenny is sadly walking around hell. He walks up to another one of hell's prisoners.

KENNY
Mph rmph rm rmph rm?

GEORGE BURNS
Snacky Smores? Why the hell would I have proofs of purchases from Snacky Smores? Beat it, kid.
Kenny moves along. He hears some voices coming from a door.
Kenny opens the door and peeps inside-

INT. SATAN'S BEDROOM - KENNY'S POV
Saddam and Satan are lying in bed.

SADDAM HUSSEIN
You just get cranky when you're tired, that's all. I told you that you shouldn't have tried to carry that futon all by yourself.

SATAN

I'm not cranky. And that futon was not too big to carry myself-
Just then, Satan hears a reporter on CNN.

TV
In war news, countries from Europe and
Asia are joining sides in the Canadian-
American War-

SADDAM HUSSEIN
-Listen butterbuns, let's make love and forget about the whole thing-

SATAN
SHHH!!!!
TV
... The death count is already on its way to 10 million with no signs of slowing down.
What started as a spat between the
United States and Canada is quickly turning into World War III-
Kenny's eyes bulge, he wants to see more, but Satan clicks off the television and sits up
in bed.

SATAN
It has come to be... The Four Horsemen are drawing nigh! The time of the prophecy is
upon us!

SADDAM HUSSEIN
Oh I love when you get all biblical
Satan. You know exactly how to turn my crank!

SATAN
No I'm being serious! Those Canadian entertainers are to be killed. It is the seventh sign.
Satan walks over to large pedestal which holds an ancient tome. Satan turns the pages as
he talks.

SATAN
Behold, the signs of my reign on earth are all falling into place! The fall of an empire-
He points to an ancient-looking picture of the death of
Ceasar.

SATAN
-The coming of a comet-
He points to a picture of a comet passing by Earth.

SATAN

Jerry Springer's movie doing more than ten million box office-
A picture of Jerry Springer holding a bunch of money.

SATAN
... . And now... .
Satan points to an ancient drawing on the wall. It looks like
Terrance and Phillip being stabbed in the head.

SATAN
The seventh sign! When the blood of these Canadians touches American soil...
It will be my time to rise!!!!!
DRAMATIC music.

SADDAM HUSSEIN
Yeah! YEAH!!! Man I'm getting so HOT!!!

SATAN
Do you always think about sex? I'm talking about some very important stuff here!

SADDAM HUSSEIN
Listen buttercup, let's make love and forget about the whole thing.

SATAN
Is sex the only thing that matters to you?
Saddam thinks for a second.

SADDAM HUSSEIN
I love you.
Satan sits with his arms crossed and a frown.

SADDAM HUSSEIN
You know I do.

SATAN
I know.

SADDAM HUSSEIN
So what do you say we shut off that light and get close, huh?
Satan reaches over and turns off the light. Everything goes pitch black. The light goes off
of Kenny's face as well.
A beat.
Then, a small moan from Satan.

SADDAM HUSSEIN
Yeah, you like that, don't you bitch?

EXT. SOUTH PARK AVENUE - DAY
Stan and Kyle are walking down South Park Avenue. Stan is reading out of a huge book.

KYLE
Does it say what the clitoris is?

STAN
All it says is that it's above the vulva... But where the hell is the vulva?

KYLE
Isn't that in Arizona or something?
Stan and Kyle walk into the middle of town, where a HUGE bonfire of Terrance and Phillip videos, posters, and Canadian items like syrup and hockey sticks are burning away.
The soldiers throw Stan's book on top of the pile, and it starts to burn.
Stan and Kyle walk up to where Cartman is standing.

STAN
What is this?

CARTMAN
They're burning all the Canadian stuff cause of the war.

STAN
That book wasn't Canadian!
Clyde, one of the kids from school, throws his Terrance and
Phillip dolls into the burning mass.
Kyle stops him on his way back.

KYLE
Dude, don't you like Terrance and Phillip anymore?

CLYDE
Of course not! We're at war! My daddy says I HATE Canadians now!
More kids line up to burn their Terrance and Phillip stuff.
Several random mothers from M. A. C. are standing in front of the bonfire with anti-Canadian signs and T-shirts. The boys' parents aren't around, but another MAC mother is leading the charge.

MAC MOTHER

**THAT'S IT! BURN EVERYTHING CANADIAN!!!
MAKE OUR COUNTRY DECENT AGAIN FOR OUR
CHILDREN!!!**
A townsperson throws Alanis Morisette albums into the fire.
Another townsperson runs up and throws in a bag of Cheesy
Poofs.

**CARTMAN
NNOOOO!!!! WHAT ARE YOU DOING?! OH, WHY
GOD, WHY?!**
Cartman falls to his knees and cries as the Cheesy Poofs burn away.

CARTMAN
This is all cause of your mom, Kyle.
She's such a bitch-

(BBBZAATT!!)
AGH!! I mean - she's such a... meanie.

KYLE
And she's getting worse...

STAN
Dude... Isn't that your brother?
Kyle looks to where a group of big, mean FIFTH GRADERS have encircled Ike.

FIFTH GRADER
Why don't you go back to your own country, CANADIAN!

FIFTH GRADER 2
Yeah, go eat some potatoes and ride donkeys!

IKE
Eee todo ba!
Kyle's eyes grow wide. He dashes over.

KYLE
Hey! Leave him alone!

FIFTH GRADER
It's just a smelly Canadian. They're like rats.

KYLE

76

He's my brother!

FIFTH GRADER
You don't look Canadian.

KYLE
He's adopted!
Kyle picks his brother up and tries to protect him.

FIFTH GRADER
Well you better get his beady eyed
Canadian ass out of America before my daddy finds him!!
The boys watch in horror as the fifth graders run over and throw more Canadian items into the fire.

KYLE
It's only a matter of time before my mom has HIM burned too!

STAN
What has the world come to? This is horrible. We're locked up, burning books, hating other people-

CARTMAN
-no Cheesy Poofs.

STAN
-No Cheesy Poofs... What the hell is happening?
DRAMATIC MUSIC begins.

KYLE
I don't know. But it has gone far enough!
I'm sick of it!
(Singing)

Something must be done!
Change has got to come around!
They're taking all our laughter and burning it to the ground!
Can't you see what this is leading to?
A world of chains and ties and glue!
We have to fight before they've taken every one!
Something must be done!

STAN

I agree! The only way to save our future is to unite and fight!
(Singing)

Something must be done!
We must take action fast!
My parents have gotten so strict they forgot they were children in the past!

CARTMAN
And my mom has become so bu-sy that she's raising heck and ignoring me
I agree that there is now a battle to be won!
Something must be done!

STAN
But what are we going to do against this entire army?

KYLE
We've gotta get the word out. We'll get on my dad's computer and use the internet! Come on you guys!
The boys proudly head down the street.

BOYS
Something must be done!
Something's gotta give!
This world has become a bitch in which we have no desire to live!
(*note- cartman gets shocked again on 'bitch')

BOYS
We've pushed it to the edge
And now the time has come!
Something's gotta change!
Something must be done!
Something must be done!!!

INT. KYLE'S HOUSE - KYLE'S DAD'S OFFICE
Kyle is at the keyboard of his dad's computer. Stan and
Cartman are waiting in the background.

KYLE
Okay... I just need to find a few private message boards...

STAN
Wait! Before we put a message out, do a search on the word 'clitoris'.

KYLE
Okay...
Kyle types in the word and hits return.

KYLE
(Reading the screen)
"Found Eight Million Pages With the Word
Clitoris"!

STAN
Wow!

KYLE
I'll just try the first one.
Kyle clicks the mouse. They wait for the screen to load.
Finally, it does.

KYLE
Dude! It's a lady giving a blow job to a horse!
Stan and Cartman rush over.

STAN
Is it Cartman's mom?

CARTMAN
Very funny!

KYLE
Hey... It IS Cartman's mom!!
Cartman looks at the screen.

CARTMAN
Oh, son of a bitch!

(ZZAP!!)
AAGHGH!! I mean, son of a biscuit!

STAN
Maybe THAT'S who your father is, Cartman!
Ike bounces in, happily.

IKE
Ber dada!

KYLE

Get out of here Ike, you're too young for this stuff!

IKE

Papa mama simi.

Ike bounces out.

CARTMAN

Come on, just get to the message board!

KYLE

I'm trying, I can't find a Canadian server... I've got to break into the main frame...

Kyle furiously hits a bunch of keys.

KYLE

Damn it! They've got an access code! I'll try to reroute the encryptions...

Kyle furiously hits a bunch more keys.

STAN

Dude, do you know what you're doing?

KYLE

No, dude, all you have to do is hit the keys really fast and say a bunch of stupid shit and it works.

Just then the screen pops up. Access Granted.

KYLE

Bingo. Okay, here we go...

(Typing)

Want to help Terrance and Phillip? Meet us for a meeting at Gladdy's barn tomorrow night...

CARTMAN

Tell 'em we'll have pie and punch.

KYLE

We're not gonna have pie and punch!

CARTMAN

More people will come if they think there'll be pie and punch!

KYLE

(Typing) pie and punch... This is Top Secret. The password is...
The boys all think...

STAN
(Dramatically)
La Resistance.
Triumphant MUSIC cue.

INT. KYLE'S ATTIC
The door to the attic pops open. Kyle shoves Ike up into the attic.

KYLE
You stay up here in the attic, Ike.
Don't make any noises or nothing, okay?

IKE
Uhh...

KYLE
Goodnight, Ike, we're all going to bed.
The door closes and it is dark.
Ike blinks. He looks out a small window, onto the street below.
A few armed soldiers walk by.
Ike pulls out a little plastic harmonica and sadly starts to play.

INT. PENTAGON - NIGHT
Tons of MILITARY PERSONNEL are running to and fro. Giant computer screens show
Canada's latest attacks.

SECRETARY OF DEFENSE
Sir! The Canadians have destroyed Des
Moines!!

PRESIDENT
How can you tell?
Everyone laughs merrily.

SECRETARY OF DEFENSE
Good one, sir!
Suddenly, a PENTAGON GUY runs up to the President, holding some papers.

PENTAGON GUY

Sir, we're tracking a signal crossing into Canadian computers! It looks like we may have a resistance movement starting...

The President grabs the papers and dashes over to Kyle's mother, who is standing there looking smug, with her arms behind her back and her chest out. She has a few military badges on her.

PRESIDENT
(Showing her the papers)
Ma'am, we're tracking a resistance...
It's probably Canadian spies!!

KYLE'S MOTHER
Well find out where that signal is coming from! Then hunt them down like dogs!
Any and all Canadian influence must be stopped at all cost!

PRESIDENT
Yes ma'am!
The President starts to run off.

KYLE'S MOTHER
And Bill?

PRESIDENT
Yes?

KYLE'S MOTHER
I'm needing lunch.

PRESIDENT
Right away, ma'am!
The president runs off.

EXT. CARTMAN'S HOUSE - NIGHT
Establishing.

RADIO ANNOUNCER (V. O.)
And so the draft will begin tomorrow, as more and more troops are needed to fight the Canadian forces...

INT. CARTMAN'S HOUSE - NIGHT
Cartman's mother is tucking him into bed.

RADIO ANNOUNCER (V. O.)

What is quickly being referred to as 'The
Great Canadian-American War' has already reached a death toll of two million.
Cartman's mother reaches over and switches off the radio.

CARTMAN'S MOTHER
Goodnight, honey.

CARTMAN
Mom... When is the war gonna be over?

CARTMAN'S MOTHER
I don't know honey. Soon we hope. You want it to end quickly, huh?

CARTMAN
Oh, I don't care, I was just asking cuz all my favorite TV shows have been replaced by
news and it's pissing me off.

CARTMAN'S MOTHER
Oh.
With that, Cartman's mother gets up-

CARTMAN
Mom...

CARTMAN'S MOTHER
Yes, hon?

CARTMAN
If you went down on a horse... You'd tell me, right?

CARTMAN'S MOTHER
Sure, hon. Goodnight.
She switches off the light, and leaves.
Cartman lies there, lit only by soft, blue moonlight and thinks.
He hears a SCRAPING noise, and looks a little scared, but then tries to close his eyes to
sleep.

CARTMAN
Go away, scary noise.
Again the SCRAPING. Cartman pops open hs eyes to see -
KENNY! He is transparent and floating above Cartman's bed.
Cartman is horrified. Too much so to even scream.
Kenny puts his hands to his mouth to try and speak, but he makes no sound.

83

Finally, Cartman lets out a piercing cry.
Cartman's mother comes running in, just as the image of Kenny disappears.

CARTMAN'S MOTHER
Eric?! Eric, what is it?!

CARTMAN
I saw him!! I saw Kenny!!
Cartman's mother looks around and sees nothing. Finally, she just cradles Cartman's fat head in her arms.

CARTMAN'S MOTHER
Oh you poor dear. You've been through so much...

CARTMAN
I bet him he couldn't set himself on fire and now he's all pissed off!!

(BZZTZT!)
AGH! I can't say pissed off?!

(BAZZTZT!!)
AGH!!
INT. HELL - DAY (MOVED)
Kenny is again snooping around. He quietly creaks Satan's door open and walks in.
Satan is in his room, looking at a map of Earth.

SATAN
The execution of Terrance and Phillip is imminent, soon all hell shall rise!!
Kenny looks scared.

SATAN
(Evil and scary)
Are you afraid, little one? Afraid for the souls of your pitiful friends that-
Suddenly, Saddam walks in carrying some bags.

SADDAM HUSSEIN
Hey Satan! I got some great new home furnishings today!
Satan rolls his eyes and sighs. His attempt to be evil to
Kenny is squashed again.

SADDAM HUSSEIN
Boy buddy Rich, it was a bitch to get something to match with that bathroom tile!
Saddam looks at Kenny.

SADDAM HUSSEIN

Oh, hey kid. Find those proofs of purchases yet? No?! Gee, whatta surprise!
Well, keep lookin!
A beat. Satan folds his arms and looks at the floor, pissed.

SATAN

Do you wanna know what I did today?
Saddam lets out a sigh.

SADDAM HUSSEIN

What did you do today Satan?

SATAN

You don't care.

SADDAM HUSSEIN

Hey fella! Relax! This whole armageddon thing has got you all stressed out. Let's make
love.

SATAN

Do you remember when you first got here?
We used to talk all night long. Until the sun came up... We would just lie in bed and
TALK.

SADDAM HUSSEIN

That's because I wanted to fuck you, dumbass! Now hows aboot you get those pants
down!

SATAN

Don't call me dumb!

SADDAM HUSSEIN

I mean cute dumb. Now bend over!
As this conversation happens, Kenny's eyes dart back and forth as if watching a tennis
match.

SATAN

How come you always want to make love to me from behind? Is it because you want to
pretend I'm somebody else?
Saddam sighs.

SADDAM HUSSEIN

Satan, your ass is gigantic and red, who am I gonna pretend you are? Helen Reddy?
A beat.

SADDAM HUSSEIN
Come on, kid. Help me with these shower curtains.
Saddam and Kenny walk out. Leaving Satan all alone with sad music playing.

SATAN
(Gently)

Sometimes I think
When I look up real high
That there's a whole world up there
And just maybe it could be mine
But then, I sink because it's here I'm supposed to stay but I don't even know how or
why its supposed to be that way-
Satan walks to his veranda.

SATAN
Up there, there is so much room
Where babies burp and flowers bloom
Everyone dreams I can dream too
Up there, Up where
The skies are ocean blue
I could be safe and live without a care... Up there
Satan walks over to a bright blue globe and spins it slowly.

SATAN
They say I don't belong
That my place is down below
Because of my beliefs I'm supposed to stay where evil is sewn
But what is evil anyway?
Is there reason to the rhyme?
Without evil there could be no good
So it must be good to be evil sometimes
Up there, there is so much room
Where babies burp and flowers bloom.
Everyone dreams I can dream too
Up there, Up where
The skies are ocean blue
I could be safe and life without a care... Up there
PULL BACK, big crane shot rising above Satan.

EXT. SMALL ABANDONED BUILDING - NIGHT
A dim light is all that is visible from inside the small building.

INT. LA RESISTANCE - NIGHT
Stan and Kyle are painting a sign on the wall 'La Resistance'.
Cartman comes running in, he looks scared.

KYLE
You're late, Cartman!

CARTMAN
I had to ride my bike here. My behind is killing me.

KYLE
Your behind?

CARTMAN
I have to say 'behind'! I get shocked if
I say 'ass-

(BBZZAATT)
OW!!!
KYLE
Did you bring the pie and punch?

CARTMAN
No you guys... Something happened... You guys wanna hear something creepy?
(Looking over each shoulder)
I don't think Kenny is dead.

STAN
What?

CARTMAN
I saw him last night!

KYLE
I know Cartman, I know. I see Kenny every day.

CARTMAN
YOU DO?!
KYLE

Sure, dude. On the face of every child, on the smile of every baby...
Kyle and Stan laugh again.

CARTMAN
Hey! I'm telling you this WAS Kenny! I think he's haunting me.

KNOCK KNOCK KNOCK!
The boys all look scared.

KYLE
Somebody's here...
The boys walk over to the door, and open the sliding panel in front of their eyes.

KYLE
Who is it?

VOICE
Uhh... I'm here for La Resistance.

KYLE
What's the password?

VOICE
Uhh... I don't know.

KYLE
Guess.

VOICE
Uhh... Bacon.

KYLE
Okay.
Kyle opens the door. The golden haired young boy from rehab stands there looking handsome and angelic.

GREGORY
Viva la Resistance.

STAN
Oh no, it's that kid.

GREGORY

This is the place--
Another kid walks up next to Gregory, it's Wendy. Stan's eyes grow wide.

STAN
Wendy?

WENDY
Stan?! YOU started La Resistance?

GREGORY
Well, apparently you have a bigger heart than we thought. Let us get this meeting underway, there are others coming.
Gregory takes Wendy's hand and pushes his way in. Stan fumes.

INT. LA RESISTANCE - LATER
Now the room is filled with a bunch of scared looking
RESISTANCE FOLLOWERS. All of whom are under the age of twelve.
The room is lit only by candlelight. And the large 'VIVA LA
RESISTANCE' banner hands on the wall.
Stan and Kyle look nervous.

STAN
Everyone be seated, please.
The kids all sit down.

KYLE
Wow, a lot of people showed up.

STAN
Yeah, so what do we say?

KYLE
I thought you had something planned.

STAN
Me?!
Stan looks out over the faces. Gregory checks his watch.

STAN
(Nervous)
Kay. Uh... Terrance and Phillip are supposed to be killed, and we think that sucks ass!!
The kids don't respond. Stan shoots a nervous look at Wendy, who is sitting next to Gregory.

89

STAN
Uhh... So we think we should prank call a bunch of policemen! We can have pizzas sent to them that they didn't order! VIVA

LA RESISTANCE!!!
Again no response. Gregory rolls his eyes.

STAN
Uhh...
Gregory stands up.

GREGORY
May I?

STAN
What?
Gregory takes Stan's place at the front of the group.

GREGORY
Terrance and Phillip are currently being held at a Canadian Internment camp two kilometers outside of town.
They are to be executed tomorrow during a star-studded USO show for the troops.
Gregory pulls a big map out of nowhere and rolls it out. Stan and Kyle can't believe it.

GREGORY
We must sneak into the camp through this duct, freeing Terrance and Phillip inside... The war is escalating, and the
American forces are preparing for a large scale attack on Canada. That means the time is now...

KYLE
Wow, dude, Wendy's new guy is smart.
Stan shoots Kyle a dirty look.

GREGORY
This is a dangerous mission, so I'll go myself.
Wendy smiles at Gregory.

STAN
No!
Everyone looks at Stan.

STAN

WE'RE going! WE started La Resistance to save Terrance and Phillip! We're going!

GREGORY

This will be very dangerous... Are you quite sure?

CARTMAN

Fuck that!

(BZZT)
AGAGH!!
STAN

We're going... Let's run through the plan!!

INT. SOUTH PARK - AMERICAN ARMY HEADQUARTERS

A huge hall is filled with hundreds of soldiers in different battalions.
We see our regulars: Mr. Garrison with a uniformed Mr. Hat,
Mr. Mackey, Jimbo and Ned, Bo, Pip, Stan's Grandfather,
Jesus, Officer Barbrady... .

JIMBO

Oh, I'm so glad there's a war again. I was gettin' worried I'd never see another one!

NED

I know what you mean.

JIMBO

And they're giving all us troops a big
USO tomorrow with celebrities and executions!
PAN OVER to Mr. Garrison.

MR. GARRISON

You look great in your new uniform Mr.
Hat.

MR. HAT

You do too, Mr. Garrison.

MR. GARRISON

Boy, I can't wait for our first shore- leave so I can go get me some poontang.
Chef sits down in a seat behind Garrison near the back.
GENERAL PLYMKIN, a gruff old army type with bug eyes, steps up to a podium and addresses the troops.

GENERAL PLYMKIN
PAY ATTENTION!
The crowd settles down.

GENERAL PLYMKIN
It's no secret that the Evil Canadian
Federation has scored major victories all over the United State. We have brought you here because you ar America's best, and last hope.
Another general leans over to Plymkin and whispers in his ear.

GENERAL PLYMKIN
Oh... Apparently you're not the best, you're simply the last. Anyway, let's strategize... Map!
A large, holographic 3-D map of South Park springs up in front of him. He walks around it pointing out things with a laser-pointer.

GENERAL PLYMKIN
Our sources have told us that the
Canadians might try to attach tomorrow's
USO show and stop us from executing
Terrance and Phillip.
He points to a spot on the 3-D map.

GENERAL PLYMKIN
Now each battalion has a specific code- name and mission. Battalion 5, raise your hands-
Chef is in Battalion 5 and dutifully raises his hand.
Then he looks around and notices to his surprise that everybody else in his section is also African American.

GENERAL PLYMKIN
You will be the all-important first defense wave, which we will call
'Operation Human Shield'.

CHEF
Hey, wait a minute...

GENERAL PLYMKIN
Now keep in mind, 'Operation Human
Shield' will suffer heavy losses. But don't lose your spirit men! Stay until the bitter end.
Battalion 14?
A bunch of white guys raise their hands.

GENERAL PLYMKIN

Right, you are 'Operation Get Behind The
Darkies'. You will follow Battalion 5 here-
He points to a spot on the 3-D map.

GENERAL PLYMKIN

-and try not to get killed for God's
Sake. Are there any questions men?
Chef raises his hand.

GENERAL PLYMKIN

Yes soldier?

CHEF

Have you ever heard of the Emancipation
Proclamation?

GENERAL PLYMKIN

I don't listen to hip-hop.
Chef scowls.

GENERAL PLYMKIN

If you somehow live, we will regroup on this hill outside--
Suddenly, the 3-D hologram starts to flicker and fizzle.

GENERAL PLYMKIN

Now what's wrong with this thing?
General Plymkin messes with the controls.

GENERAL PLYMKIN

Fucking windows 98!
General Plymkin has pulled the plug. He stands there with the cord in his hands.

GENERAL PLYMKIN
GET GATES IN HERE!!!
BILL GATES walks in, escorted by two MILITARY GUARDS.

GENERAL PLYMKIN
YOU TOLD US WINDOWS 98 WOULD BE FASTER
AND MORE EFFICIENT WITH BETTER ACCESS TO
THE INTERNET!!!
BILL GATES
It is faster, over five million--

93

Plymkin pulls out a gun and shoots him in the head. Gates falls to the floor, dead.

GENERAL PLYMKIN
Alright men, get lots of rest, and prepare thyselves for battle!

INT. LA RESISTANCE - NIGHT
In the dead of night, the kids are all in a circle discussing the plan.

GREGORY
... after you clear this zone here, rendezvous behind this ridge where
Terrance and Phillip should be held.

KYLE
Gotcha.

GREGORY
You are indeed brave, but you will need someone who's done this sort of thing before.
MOLE!
Suddenly, a bump in the ground starts to move forward, leaving a trail behind it. (like
bugs bunny before he pops out)
The bump comes to a stop at the children's feet and out pops
THE MOLE. He is a very bitter little nine year old French kid with a THICK French
accent.

VOICE
Oui?

GREGORY
Thank you for coming, Mole.

THE MOLE
So... We must free more Canadian prizoners?

KYLE
Yeah, I guess.

THE MOLE
America... She iz a beetch that sheets on her own children.
Stan and Kyle look at each other confused.

GREGORY
This is the Mole. He will accompany you to the prison where Terrance and Phillip are.
He is an expert in covert operations and a lifelong fighter for freedom.

THE MOLE
Freedom... It's like cow's urine poured down your troat. You wonder 'Do I want this?' I'm thersty... But it's urine.
Everyone stares at The Mole.

GREGORY
Good luck Stan, I'll make sure Wendy is... kept safe?
Stan gets pissed.

KYLE
Give me Terrance and Phillip or give me death!!!

OTHERS
YEA!!!
Now, Gregory breaks into song. His voice is absolutely gorgeous and deep. He puts his hand on Stan's shoulder.

GREGORY
God has smiled upon you this day
The fate of a nation in your hands...
Stan and Kyle look at each other. They can't believe how good this guy's voice is. Wendy appears enthralled.

GREGORY
As brothers and sisters we unite
And behind you we shall fight!
Until only the most righteous belief stands!
The music builds. Gregory gets up on a soapbox.

GREGORY
Do you see the distant flames? they bellow in the night
Fight in all our names
For what we know is right
And if you all get shot and cannot carry on
Though you die, La Resistance lives on!

KYLE
What? Shot?
Kyle and the boys look a little worried, as other kids join in the song.

KIDS
You might get stabbed in the head by a dagger or a sword

95

You might be burned to death or skinned alive or worse!

GREGORY
But when they torture you
You will not feel a need to run
For though you die, La Resistance
Lives on!

KIDS
Do you hear the beating drum?
It is our hearts all joined to one
It is the music of our souls knowing we have much to overcome!
As THE SONG CONTINUES we-

CUT TO:
EXT. USO SHOW - NIGHT
The MAC Mothers are on a stage, preparing two electric chairs.

KYLE'S MOTHER
Something must be done!
Tomorrow it will be!
We're going to execute this threat to our democracy!
All the mothers join in as they decorate the chairs with
American flags. Kenny's mother is counting money she has made from selling t-shirts.

M. A. C. MOTHERS
And after that our kids will be safe from all the Canadian scum!
The time is now the time is here
Tomorrow something will be done!
The song still CONTINUES as we

CUT TO:
EXT. HELL - CONTINUOUS
Satan stands on his veranda.

SATAN
I want to be part of that world!
But if only I had the strength to go without HIM...
If only I had the strength to leave him behind...
Get on with my life in that world...
Start over as part of that world...

CUT TO:

INT. MILITARY BARRACKS - CONTINUOUS
The soldiers, including Garrison, Mackey, Ned and Jimbo are in their bunks.

SOLDIERS
Tomorrow we face our destiny!
Tomorrow we fight to keep our country free!
Death to Canada! Death to them all!
Like our forefathers we shall answer the call!
PAN DOWN to Chef's bunk where he is lying naked with a hot chick. As usual, Chef sings a song that has absolutely no relevance to what's going on.

CHEF
(Stroking woman's arm)

Baby your thighs sparkle like diamonds
Baby your butt is tender like the night
I can see by the look in your pants that you want to treat me right.
I'll whisper sweet nothings in your cleavage
And you can kiss me gently with your tongue
And I'll make love to you so deeply
That you'll feel pressure clear up to your lungs.
Meanwhile, the soldiers continue their song.

SOLDIERS
Something must be done!
Something's gotta give!
Tomorrow we will be free or we will no longer live!

CUT TO:
INT. MILITARY PRISON - CONTINUOUS
Terrance and Phillip are chained to the wall in a dark, dirty prison cell. Two armed American soldiers are torturing
Terrance and Phillip with hot irons, as Terrance and Phillip sing-

TERRANCE & PHILLIP
Shut your fucking face Unclefucka!
You're an ass raping cock sucking
Unclefucka!!!

CUT TO:
EXT. LA RESISTANCE - CONTINUOUS
The kids are all gathered together, finishing their song.
One kid grabs a large flag and starts swirling it around.

KIDS
Let it echo through the night!
Let it reach the ears of everyone!
Though we die
La Resistance lives on!
Though we die
La Resistance lives onnnn!!!!!
Ah- AHHHH!!!

FADE OUT.
EXT. SOUTH PARK AVENUE
All the South Park men are in the rank and file marching down the street.

OFFICER
(Singing)
I don't know but I've been told-

SOLDIERS
I DON'T KNOW BUT I'VE BEEN TOLD!
They pass Kyle's house.

INT. KYLE'S HOUSE - ATTIC
Ike watches the soldiers march from his little attic window.

OFFICER (O. S.)
Canadian pussy is mighty cold!

SOLDIERS (O. S.)
CANADIAN PUSSY IS MIGHTY COLD!
Ike blinks. Does he understand them? he picks up a small book and starts to write in it.

INT. HELL - DAY
Satan paces back and forth in hell.

SATAN
This is it! World War Three is at hand!
The millennium nears!
Satan crosses to one of his small demons.

SATAN
Prepare the minions for the rising of
Gothos!

The demon dashes off.

SADDAM HUSSEIN
This is so exciting! Let's fuck!
Satan sighs and bows his head.

SATAN
This is the millennium, Saddam! This is
Armageddon! There's more to life than sex!

SADDAM HUSSEIN
Hey, relax guy!

SATAN
Well I just want you to be impressed with what I do. I want you to respect my MIND.

SADDAM HUSSEIN
I DO respect your mind! It turns me on!
It makes me wanna fuck the shit out of you! Don't you see?

MUSIC BEGINS.
SADDAM HUSSEIN
(Singing)

Hey guy, relax, put out
You gotta put out for me!
I'm just a man with needs
And right now I need your generosity!
I love your eyes, your nose and lips
So drop those pants and do some dips
Come on guy, you gotta relax relax, put out for me!
Kenny looks confused.

SATAN
What if I, don't wanna put out?
That's all you ever say
Relax put out
I'm a living creature, I have feelings too, I don't need this abuse from you-

SADDAM HUSSEIN
Hey, guy, relax, put out!
You gotta relax, shut your mouth-
Baby I'd do anything for ya!

Now don't make me smack you in the eye like last time-
Kenny keeps watching as Saddam throws on a Shakey's hat and does a quick softshoe.
Satan rolls his eyes.

SADDAM HUSSEIN
I get what I want, and what I want is for youuuuu toooo put oooooout!!!
Saddam finishes the song and Satanhangs his head.

SATAN
What if I just left?

SADDAM HUSSEIN
Where're you gonna go, bitch? Besides, you know that if you left me, I'd hunt you down
and kill you, right? I'm gonna go grab a drink.
Saddam leaves. Satan looks about to cry, but then notices
Kenny still standing there.

SATAN
What are you doing?! Get on with your misery!

KENNY
Mph rmph rm rmph rm?

SATAN
Him? I don't know... He can be nice... sometimes.

KENNY
Mph rmph rm rmph rm.

SATAN
What do you mean?! I could leave him if I wanted to!

KENNY
Mph rm. Rmph rm rmph rm.
Satan lowers his head. Slowly he starts to cry. Kenny walks over and pats him on the
back.

EXT. MILITARY COMPOUND
Tents and makeshift buildings are lined up against the mountains. Jeeps and Tanks buzz
to and fro.
There's a huge stage which is set up with thousands of seats.
There's a giant banner reading "USO SHOW TONIGHT!!!!!"
Loads of soldiers file into their seats.

ANNOUNCER
Alright you men! The USO show is about to start!!
The military men go wild.

ANNOUNCER
Get ready for loads of entertainment and fabulous celebrities! To be followed immediately by the swift and nasty execution of Terrance and Elroy!
The crowd goes crazy again.

EXT. INTERNMENT CAMP - BEHIND THE USO SHOW - DUSK
Right out of Nazi Germany. Barbed wire, guards, the whole bit.

ANGLE ON BOYS
They are on their backs, shimmying along the ground underneath the blanket of razor-wire that is set up around the camp.
The Mole uses the bolt-cutters to cut the wire as he goes, clearing a path for Stan, Kyle and Cartman.

THE MOLE
Be careful not to touch this wire-
A wire catches on Cartman's arm and SNAPS against his face.

CARTMAN
OW! MOTHERFUCKER!
BZZAAAAT!!!
CARTMAN
FUC-
Stan shoves his hand over Cartman's mouth, leaving Cartman to cuss bloody murder into Stan's glove.

CARTMAN
MPHMPH MPHMPHMPH!!!
BZAAT!
CARTMAN
MMMPPPHHH!!!
Finally they clear the fence and lie down in view of the camp.

THE MOLE
It sounds like the USO show has started.
We have precious little time...
Kyle looks at the horrible concentration camp.

101

KYLE
Oh my God...

THE MOLE
God? ... Let me tell you something about
God... He is ze biggest bitch of zem all.
Kyle looks at The Mole, oddly.

STAN
How are we ever gonna find them?
The Mole whips out some night vision goggles.

ANGLE ON INTERMENT CAMP THROUGH NIGHT VISION GOGGLES
The Mole inspects the camp. He sees a guard on a guard tower. Then he pans over to a
bunch of Canadians standing in a line in rags.
The Mole quickly clicks the magnification to high so we see the saddened faces of the
Canadians.

KYLE
Do you see them? Do you see Terrance and
Phillip?

THE MOLE
No. Zey must have zem inside. We will have to dig.

KYLE
That's gonna take a long time!

THE MOLE
Time? Did time matter to the
Revolutionists who were forced to eat their own shit while dying in the dungeons of ze
King?
The boys think.

EXT. USO SHOW - DAY
Helicopters zoom over the makeshift stage like the USO show in Apocalypse Now.
Groups of soldiers cheer as a helicopter approaches the landing platform and touches
down. The US army men cheer.
The mothers take the stage, and Kyle's mother speaks into the microphone. Behind her is
a huge American flag. She is wearing an army helmet. This is right out of 'Patton'.

KYLE'S MOTHER
Ladies and gentlemen of the American war effort, we salute you!

A big cheer goes through the crowd. Kyle's mother feels the power, and lifts her head high. She starts to pace back and forth on the stage as she speaks, becoming more and more
Pattonlike.

KYLE'S MOTHER
Tomorrow you will be risking your lives so that our children will have a better future... God bless you men. And God bless this filth free nation. Many of you will die. Die like blood bathed pigs. So tonight, we at MAC present a NIGHT OF A
HUNDRED STARS! Now without further ado, I give you...
Out of the helicopter emerge a battalion of the best and brightest stars that the American show biz industry has to offer.

KYLE'S MOTHER
Pint size pixie and darling of the indie movie scene, Winona Ryder!
She gestures grandly to the helicopter where Winona Ryder emerges and runs to center stage and waves to the audience.
She looks like a strung out coke addict; because she is.

WINONA RYDER
Hi guys! I'm T. V. 's Winona Ryder!
One guy claps.

WINONA RYDER
I want you all to know I'm super psyched to be here today. You guys rock. What you're doing for our country so sooo cool. It's so real. I've been acting since I was twelve and I can't distinguish between make believe and real life.
Winona falls down. But gets back up immediately.

WINONA RYDER
And then I confuse me real life with my big-screen one. And sure, people get hurt, and I'm sorry about that but
Christ, look at me. It's not my fault that I can get any guy I want. And that's reality to me. But you guys... wow. I mean, war, man. Fucking war. It doesn't get any more real-- Now, this one goes out to you.
She cues the band which has been assembled from the same helicopter. Jazz music starts up.
It's 'New York, New York'. The troops look confused.

WINONA RYDER
You know what I'm gonna do for you now, don't you?
'New York, New York' continues to play.

103

WINONA RYDER
WRONG!
(Singing)

The bells are ringin'
For me and my gal!
The birds are singin'
For me and my gal!-

INT. UNDERGROUND TUNNEL - BELOW THE USO SHOW
The mole is digging frantically while the boys follow on all fours. Cartman holds a flashlight.

CARTMAN
Dude, this is seriously lame. I didn't know we were gonna get all dirty and stuff.

THE MOLE
Sheet!

STAN
What is it?

THE MOLE
Bedrock! I cannot dig any further in zis direction!

STAN
We're going to die here like baby mice who have had no milk in days. Dry up into crunchy little pinkies.
The boys stare.
A beat.

THE MOLE
Or, we can dig UP.
The mole starts digging up towards the ground.

EXT. INSIDE THE PRISON CAMP
Mole pops his head out of the ground. Immediately, a search light passes over the hole.

THE MOLE
Sheet!
Mole ducks, just avoiding the light.
Slowly, the boys' heads appear from the hole.

The whole camp is in front of them. There is a HUGE barbedwire fence on one side (the side they just dug from) A dozen armed guards with huge Dobermans patrol the grounds with
Howitzers. It doesn't look good.

THE MOLE
Move! Move!
One by one, The Mole, Stan, Kyle, and Cartman pop out of the ground, and run for a nearby building. Once at the building, they all duck to avoid the search lights.

THE MOLE
Okay.... . The Americans must be holding
Terrance and Phillip in one of those bunkers. We will split up here. Let's synchronize watches!
The others look at each other.

KYLE
We don't have watches.
A beat.

THE MOLE
You don't have watches?

STAN
Dude, you didn't say anything about watches.

THE MOLE
What do you think this is kid? Lick
Barney the Dinosaur's pussy fucking kiddie hour? Huh? This is real life with consequences you take to the grave!

KYLE
Dude, we don't have watches.

THE MOLE
Sheet. Did you bring ze mirror?

STAN
Got it.

THE MOLE
And ze rope?

STAN
Check.

THE MOLE
And the butfor?

KYLE
What's a butfor?

THE MOLE
For pooping, silly.
A beat... Then mole takes a long drag off his cigarette and slowly blows the smoke.

THE MOLE
Now listen carefully. Stan and Kyle, you stand watch here and await my return. If any guards come by, make a sound like a dying giraffe.

KYLE
What's a dying giraffe sound like?

THE MOLE
(Putting his hands to his mouth)
Gwpaapa. Gwpaapa.

KYLE
Kay.
The Mole turns to Cartman.

THE MOLE
Cartman, over zere, is the electrical box. You must sneak over zere and shut it off before I return with Terrance and
Phillip or the alarms will sound and I will be shot full of holes. Got it?

CARTMAN
Okay.

THE MOLE
You MUST shut off the power, this is VERY
IMPORTANT do you understa-

CARTMAN
**I HEARD YOU THE FIRST TIME! I'M NOT LOU
FERIGNO FOR PETE'S SAKE!**

Cartman storms off.

THE MOLE
I will tunnel my way into ze buildings, and find ze prisoners.
The Mole starts to dig.

KYLE
Be careful, dude.

THE MOLE
Careful? Was my mother careful when she stabbed me in the heart with a clothes hanger while I was still in ze womb?
And with that, The Mole quickly starts to tunnel his way underground.

STAN
Damn, dude, that kid is fucked up.

EXT. STAGE - NIGHT
Back on stage at the USO show. Winona Ryder is just finishing up her song.

WINONA RYDER
(Singing)

... . It's a hell of a TOWN! And that's my New York Melodyyyyyy!!!!
The band finishes with a flourish. Winona takes a bow.
One person in the entire audience claps.

KYLE'S MOTHER
Let's hear it again for the one and only
Winona Ryder!!!
The same guy claps again.

ONE CLAPPING GUY
We love you, Winona!
Everybody else in the audience just stares at him.

KYLE'S MOTHER
Next up we have a special treat...
Please welcome, direct from Vegas- BIG

GAY AL'S BIG GAY EXPERIENCE!!!
The place goes wild as Big Gay Al walks out on stage. Winona fumes in the wings.

RANDOM SOLDIER
This guy is the coolest!

RANDOM SOLDIER 2
Totally man!
The back curtain goes up to reveal a tropical jungle set complete with a waterfall, hippos, monkeys and hundreds of colorfully dressed dancers.

BIG GAY AL
How we all feeling tonight?!
Between the cheering, we hear a throng of "Happy!". Now the place is rocking!!
Everybody loves Big Gay Al!
Winona can't believe it.

BIG GAY AL
I can't hear you...

CROWD
Happy!!!

BIG GAY AL
Friends, you know why I'm here... I'm here to teach TOLERANCE!!
The crowd cheers.

BIG GAY AL
I'm here to say that we're all PEOPLE under God, and we should embrace, and accept our differences!!
The crowd cheers louder.

BIG GAY AL
And that means we should LOVE CANADIANS

TOO!!
The entire place goes incredibly quiet.
You can hear a pin drop.
Silence...
Deafening silence...

BIG GAY AL
JUST KIDDING!! FUCK 'EM!!!
Slow music swells in. Big Gay Al saunters around the stage and starts to sing.

BIG GAY AL

(Singing)

Bombs are flying
People are dying
Children are crying
Politicians are lying too
Cancer is killing
Texaco is spilling
The whole world's gone to hell
But how are you?
Suddenly, Big Gay Al is wearing a big feathery outfit and all his dancers dash to his side.

BIG GAY AL
I'm super! Thanks for asking!
All things considered I'm doing super
I must say!
Very peachee
Nothing bugs me
'Cause everything is super when you're
-don't you think I look cute in this hat?
The crowd is absolutely confused.

BIG GAY AL
I'm so sorry, Mr. Cripple
But I just can't feel bad for you right now
Because I'm feeling so insanely super
That even seeing you in that chair can't bring me down!

EXT. INTERNMENT CAMP - ANOTHER AREA
Cartman is by himself, slowly moving from building to building. He is scared out of his mind.

CARTMAN
(Imitating the Mole)
Shut of ze Power, Cartman. Zis is very important, Cartman... Stupid British piece of shi-

(BAZZT!)
OW!
He approaches the electrical box. Just as he's about to open it, two armed AMERICAN SOLDIERS round the corner. Cartman gets scared and hides in the shadows. The soldiers continue walking...

AMERICAN SOLDIER

Dude, if I was gay, I'd be just like Big
Gay AL!

AMERICAN SOLDIER 2
Me too!!
... And pass a terrified Cartman.

EXT. INTERNMENT CAMP - STAN AND KYLE'S AREA
The boys are waiting, bored, for The Mole to return.

KYLE
I don't think he's coming back, dude.
Just then, we hear The Mole return from his hole. He is carrying the ticket guy from the movie theater.

TICKET GUY
Oh thank you! Thank you for getting me out of there!! They locked me up for selling movie tickets to minors!

THE MOLE
Is this one of zem?

KYLE
No! That's not Terrance or Phillip!

THE MOLE
Oh... Alright, back you go.
The Mole takes the Ticket Guy back through the hole.

TICKET GUY
No! Please! I don't want to go back!!
The boys sit back down and wait again.

EXT. USO SHOW/STAGE - CONTINUOUS
Meanwhile, Big Gay Al's song continues-

BIG GAY AL
I'm super! Thanks for asking!
All things considered I'm doing better than okay!
Feeling peaches nothing bugs me
Everything is super when you're
-don't you think I look cute in this hat and my little shoes and this matching tie that
I got at

Merv's?

The chorus guys all pick Big Gay Al up and dance around with him on stage.

CHORUS
He's super! Thanks for asking!
All things considered he is better than okay!
And it's peachee, nothing bugs him
Everything is super when you're-
Let's fight fight fight against
Canada today!!!!!!

The song ends and everyone erupts into applause.

INT. HELL - DAY
Satan is looking into a large, oracle-like ball. Saddam isn't around, but a few demons and Kenny are hanging out.

SATAN

The execution is going to happen any moment... We must prepare.
The demons make excited noises.

KENNY
Mph rmph rm!

SATAN

Get everyone in hell ready. When the blood of Terrance and Phillip spills, the day is ours!
Two of the demons head for Satan's room.

SATAN
No! Not Saddam. Don't wake him... Uh...
I'll tell him...
Satan walks to the bedroom.

EXT. INTERNMENT CAMP - ELECTRICAL BOX AREA
Cartman approaches the electrical box nervously -- looking all around for soldiers.
He opens the door to the electrical box and sees a large switch labeled ON and OFF. He reaches to turn off the switch when he feels a tap on his shoulder.
Cartman jumps.

CARTMAN
Agh!!!
Then turns and karate-chops in one spastic flurry to see -

KENNY!!

CARTMAN
Son of a gun! HECK!
Kenny's ghost is again floating in front of Cartman. Kenny again struggles to speak.

CARTMAN
GO AWAY, KENNY! IT'S NOT MY GOSH DARN
FAULT!
KENNY
Mph rmprmmh rm!!

CARTMAN
I don't have proofs of purchases from
Snacky Smores, Kenny!

KENNY
MPH RMPH RMPH RMPH RM!!!
CARTMAN
AGAGAH!!
Cartman runs off, leaving the power completely on.

INT. KYLE'S HOUSE - ATTIC - NIGHT
Ike is still just sitting quietly in the dark attic.
Suddenly, the attic door bursts open!

AMERICAN SOLDIER
Found one!
Other soldiers file into the attic and grab Ike by the arms.

AMERICAN SOLDIER
Yep, that's a Canadian alright.

IKE
Sibi mammama.
The American Soldier picks up Ike.

AMERICAN SOLDIER
So, thought you could hide from us, did you?! Take him away!
The soldiers drag Ike down the stairs.

AMERICAN SOLDIER 2
Sir, look at this!
(Holding up a book)
He was writing some kind of diary...

112

AMERICAN SOLDIER
Diary? What does it say?

AMERICAN SOLDIER 2
(Reading)
Cookie monster. Banana.
Sweeping, moving MUSIC STING.

EXT. INTERNMENT CAMP - STAN AND KYLE'S AREA
Kyle is patiently awaiting Mole's return.

KYLE
Damn it! Come on, Mole we're running out of time!
Kyle spins around when he hears someone coming.
But it's only Cartman. He's panting heavily.

CARTMAN
You guys! Seriously! You guys!

KYLE
What Cartman?!

CARTMAN
Kenny! I saw Kenny again!

STAN
Oh, brother.

KYLE
Did you shut the alarm off, Cartman?
Cartman stops breathing heavily and thinks.

KYLE
Cartman?!

CARTMAN
Whoops.
Just then, all the alarms in the place go off.

KYLE
Oh shit!
From the distance, the boys hear gunshots.

Suddenly, the Mole pops out of the hole. The boys see that
The Mole has been shot up badly.

THE MOLE
Ze alarms! Zey went off!

CARTMAN
Yeah... That was my bad, sorry.
As SHOUTS and RUNNING FOOTSTEPS draw closer, The Mole lays down and begins
to die in Kyle's arms.

THE MOLE
Please... Do not let ze resistance die...
Gentle MUSIC begins.

THE MOLE
Now the light, she fades
And darkness closes in
But I will find strength
I will find pride within
Because although I die
Our freedom will be won
Though I die
Ze Resistance
Lives on...
The Music fades away, as the Mole coughs up some blood.

THE MOLE
It's so very cold...

KYLE
We can't leave without you!

THE MOLE
It's okay, I am done for.

KYLE
No, I mean WE CAN'T LEAVE WITHOUT YOU - we don't know where the hell we
are!!
The Mole coughs up more blood.

THE MOLE
Where is your God when you need him?

Where is your beautiful, merciful faggot now?
The Mole dies.

KYLE
SHIT!
VOICE
FREEZE!!
The boys look up to see three large MARINES pointing guns at them.
Stan makes a run for it. He dashes off at full speed.

KYLE
Run, Stan!!
One of the soldiers fires at him. PWANG! PWANG! But Stan disappears into the night.

PENTAGON GUY
Forget him! The night will swallow him up.

MARINE
You are under arrest! Cuff 'em!

KYLE
What?

PENTAGON
So THIS must be the resistance the pentagon has been tracking!

CARTMAN
Oh, son of a bitch...

EXT. USO SHOW - NIGHT
Kyle's mother, and the other mothers of MAC, take the stage again.

KYLE'S MOTHER
And now, for our big finale, the MOMENT

YOU HAVE ALL BEEN WAITING FOR!!!
Terrance and Phillip are wheeled out onto the stage.

TERRANCE
Oh, Phillip. This cannot be good.

PHILLIP
I know, Terrance. This is quite the shitstorm we've found ourselves in this time.

From the other side, Kyle's mom appears with a couple of official looking military people. The crowd cheers.

KYLE'S MOM
It is my pleasure to present to you, THE

EXECUTION OF TERRANCE AND PHILLIP!!!
The crowd cheers.

KYLE'S MOM
Strap them in!
Terrance and Phillip are then greeted by the EXECUTIONER, donned in a black hood.
The scary giant Executioner grabs Terrance and Phillip and puts them into electric chairs.

KYLE'S MOM
Today is a great day for democracy!
The crowd cheers.
The Executioner steps up to the throw switch.

TERRANCE
Phillip, this is worse than that trip to
Quebec City when I fell asleep in that disco.

PHILLIP
I know, Terrance. I know.

EXT. SOMEWHERE IN SOUTH PARK - NIGHT
LONG SHOT of a desolate, dark area.
It has started to rain. Stan trudges through the wilderness looking tired and scared.

STAN
Hello? Where the hell am I? Is anybody here?
A few wolf HOWLS sound in the distance. Stan walks on.

STAN
MARCO!!!
No answer.

STAN
MARCO!!!
No answer. Stan stumbles a bit.

STAN

Dude, weak... Can't go on... Dizzy...

Stan falls to the ground. His face plops in the rainy mud and his head smacks against a rock.

Stan is out cold.

Just then, a strange sound emerges. It is like a pulsating

WOBBLE. Stan slowly awakes, picks up his head and shines his flashlight around.

STAN

What is that?

The sound gets louder. Stan shines his flashlight on something that is huge and throbbing.

STAN

OH MY GOD!!!

EXT. STAGE - NIGHT

Kyle's mother approaches Terrance and Phillip.

KYLE'S MOM

Gentlemen, do you have any last words?

PHILLIP

Last words? Let's see... How aboot "GET

ME THE FUCK OUT OF THIS CHAIR". How's that for last words?

Kyle's mom nods to the Executioner.

GENERAL PLYMKIN

WAIT!!

General Plymkin walks out next to Kyle's mother.

GENERAL PLYMKIN

We have just captured some Canadian

Sympathizers!

The crowd cheers. Kyle's mother smiles.

KYLE'S MOTHER

We will execute them along with Terrance and Phillip for your viewing pleasure!

Another cheer. The mothers are all very pleased. That is, until they see Kyle and Cartman brought out to the stage at gunpoint.

KYLE'S MOTHER

Kyle?!

CARTMAN'S MOTHER

Eric?

117

KYLE
Hi, ma.

GENERAL PLYMKIN
We also have a Canadian SPY who was hiding out in South Park!!
Now Ike is brought out at gunpoint.

KYLE'S MOTHER
Ike?!
Kyle's mother rushes over to General Plymkin.

KYLE'S MOTHER
General... These are OUR CHILDREN!

GENERAL PLYMKIN
They are Canadian sympathizers and they must be dealt with accordingly!

STAN'S MOTHER
But they're CHILDREN!
Cartman walks over to where Terrance and Phillip are strapped into their chairs.

CARTMAN
Dude! Terrance and Phillip! Wow! Can I get your autographs?!

TERRANCE
Sure, tubby, just as soon as we're killed.

KENNY'S MOTHER
We can't kill these kids!

GENERAL PLYMKIN
Listen mothers, YOU'RE the ones that started all this. Don't get all emotional

NOW!
STAN'S MOTHER
But we're doing all this to help our children's futures!

CARTMAN'S MOTHER
Yes, I think shooting our children would adversely affect their futures.

KYLE'S MOTHER
No... The General is right.

KYLE
MOM!!!
KYLE'S MOTHER
Boobie... This is the only way you're ever going to learn. I have an opportunity here to teach you about consequences.

STAN'S MOTHER
Sheila, you're going to far! Those are
YOUR children!

KYLE'S MOTHER
YES! AND I WILL NOT ALLOW MY CHILDREN TO
BE RUINED BY SMUT!!
(To Kyle)
I am sorry young man, but I have had it up to here! STRAP THEM IN!
She walks away.

KYLE
YOU GOTTA BE FUCKING KIDDING ME!!
KYLE'S MOTHER
KYLE BROVLOFSKI, YOU WATCH YOUR
LANGUAGE!!
EXT. IN THE MIDDLE OF NOWHERE - NIGHT
Stan is still lying in mud, but now he lies before a HUGE, pulsating, organic looking thing that belongs in the X-Files.
It's the size of a small building.
The massive thing starts to glow. Stan looks weak and afraid.

BIG THING
Be not afraid...
Stan trembles.

STAN
(Weakly)
What...

BIG THING
Behold my glory.

STAN
What... are you?

BIG THING
I am the clitoris.
Stan's eyes grow wide. MUSIC starts to swell up.

STAN
The clitoris?! I DID IT!! I FOUND THE

CLITORIS!!
BIG THING
Stan, your friends need you. They are in trouble and you must help them.

STAN
Wait, you're supposed to tell me how to get Wendy to like me.

BIG THING
There are more important matters right now...

STAN
NO WAY, DUDE! I'VE LOOKED ALL OVER FOR
YOU, AND NOW YOU HAVE TO TELL ME HOW TO
GET WENDY TO LIKE ME!!
BIG THING
Dude, she's eight years old, just get her some ice cream or something.

STAN
Of COURSE!! Ice cream!!

BIG THING
Now go, your friends are in danger... The
USO show is a mile east of here, just over that ridge. The clitoris has spoken.
The clitoris fades, and just as it does, all the kids of La
Resistance come running into frame. Wendy and Gregory are with them as well.

WENDY
Stan! Stan are you okay?!

STAN
Wendy?

GREGORY
I see you failed in your mission.
Terrance and Phillip must be dead by now.
Wendy bends down to pick up Stan.

WENDY
Come on Stan, we have to hurry. The
Canadian forces are about to attack!!
Wendy pulls Stan up off the ground and slings his arm around her.

EXT. USO SHOW - NIGHT
A drummer plays as the execution begins.

GENERAL PLYMKIN
We begin with Terrance and Phillip!!!
Throw the switch!!!
The executioner throws the switch and Terrance and Phillip start to fry. Kyle, Cartman and Ike, in their chairs, look horrified.

KYLE'S MOTHER
Goodbye, bastards!
Near death, Terrance cranks out a weak fart. Terrance and
Phillip both laugh weakly but merrily.

TERRANCE
Take that, bitch.
As Terrance and Phillip fry, they scream out:

PHILLIP/TERRANCE
FREEEEEEDOMMMMMM!!!
Suddenly, FWWOOOMMM!!! A Bomb lands in the middle of the army. BLAM!! It explodes with incredible force, sending dead bodies in all directions.
Canadian military planes zoom overhead! It's a full scale attack!!
From a HIGH ANGLE we see the soldiers all scatter like bugs in every direction.

MR. GARRISON
THE CANADIANS ARE ATTACKING!! RUN FOR
YOUR LIVES!!
FWWOOMM!!! BLAMM!! Another explosion! Everybody just starts screaming and shooting in every direction. Total and complete mayhem.
One explosion knocks out the electricity, and Terrance and
Phillip stop drying.
The electricity runs along a wire, across the stage, and right up Cartman's leg. Cartman starts frying horribly.

KYLE
CARTMAN!

CARTMAN
(Frying)

WAGAGAHGHGH!! YOU GUYS!!! SERIOUSLY!!!
PHILLIP
What's going on Terrance?

TERRANCE
Canada is saving us!!
Finally, Cartman is blown clear of the electricity. Kyle picks him up and starts to run along with Ike.

INT. HELL - SATAN'S BEDROOM
Satan opens the door to find Saddam sleeping happily in his cozy bed. He is only wearing little black g-string panties.

SATAN
(Whispering)
Have you finished?
Now we see that Kenny is standing at the foot of the bed. He holds a gasoline can, and has just finished pouring the last drops underneath the bed.

KENNY
Mph mph.

SATAN
Then move out of the way.
Kenny walks over next to Satan. Satan pulls out a book of matches.

SATAN
I must be strong... I must be strong...
Satan tries to light the match. It won't light.

SATAN
Damn it...
Finally, the match lights. Satan holds it up-

SATAN
Goodbye, Saddam...
-and throws it onto the bed.

SATAN
Come on!

Saddam burns to a crisp and Satan and Kenny run out.

EXT. USO SHOW - DAY
People run screaming in all directions as a full scale attack has broken out. Gunfire, explosions and dead bodies fly all around.

JIMBO
Ned! Behind you!
Ned whips around and mows down a line of Canadians. But one
Canadian makes it through, and sticks his bayonet through
Ned's neck.
Blood gushes from Ned's neck as he collapses.

JIMBO
NED!!! NOOOOOOO!!!!!
FWWOOM!! BLAMMM!!! The boys runs as fast as they can amidst the explosions.

CARTMAN
HOLY SHIT!
(Zap)

AGHAGHGAH!!
Now when the V-chip shocks Cartman, we can actually see the blue current swirl around his body.

CARTMAN
HEY! THIS V-CHIP IS GETTING ALL SCREWY!!
General Plymkin has followed his men into the trench, where explosions and gunfire fly all around. He pulls out a walkie talkie as his men die all around him.

GENERAL PLYMKIN
ALRIGHT MEN!!! FALL INTO FORMATION!
"HUMAN SHIELD" UP FRONT THEN "OPERATION
GET BEHIND THE DARKIES"!!!
They all fall in. A phalanx of black men, Chef included in them, walk out in front of a bunch of white guys.

GENERAL PLYMKIN
REMEMBER, HUMAN SHIELD! PROTECT OUR
TANKS AND PLANES, TOO!
Just then, over a ridge in front of them, a line of Canadian tanks appears. The tanks are lined up 3 deep. Behind them is a line of missile launchers. General Plymkin's jaw drops.

GENERAL PLYMKIN
Holy Mother of Johosephat...
The black guys all look at each other nervously.

EXT. BATTLEFIELD
The boys run through the chaos. Body parts and scrapnel fly here and there.
A bloody soldier suddenly stumbles and falls in front of the boys holding a massive head wound.

KYLE
Hey! It's Mr. Garrison!!
Garrison lies on the ground, coughing up blood.

MR. GARRISON
Children... Take Mr. Hat... Please... Get him out of here...
Garrison takes Mr. Hat off his hand and gives it to Cartman.
Just then, Garrison goes limp.
Cartman looks at the Mr. Hat in his hand and scowls. The boys run from the battle.
They pass the American troops, where all the black guys are standing in a human shield around the white guys.

CHEF
Alright, squad... JUST LIKE I TOLD YOU...

ONE!!
The Canadian tanks take aim.

CHEF
TWO!
The Canadian tanks fire.

CHEF
THREE!!
All the black guys suddenly jump out of the way, leaving the whites completely exposed.

GENERAL PLYMKIN
What the-
The tank fire hits the army, blowing all the white soldiers to smithereens, including Ned and Jimbo.

BLACK SOLDIER
GREAT PLAN, CHEF!
CHEF

124

Operation Human Shield my ASS!

EXT. SOUTH PARK - DAY
From an EXTREME WIDE SHOT, we see all the forces on both sides exchange firepower. The Canadian National anthem can be heard in the distance.
We see Mr. Mackey looking like a natural born killer. He shoots like a maniac into the Canadians. He wounds one and then marches over to the wriggling body with a knife.

MR. MACKEY
Die Canadian, mmkay?!
And he drives the knife into the Canadian's chest.
But then, suddenly, another Canadian Soldier appears out of nowhere, and blows a hole through Mackey's chest.

MR. MACKEY
Mkay-
Mackey falls to the ground, dead. Just then Big Gay Al runs through the frame, we FOLLOW him as he skips his way around gunfire.

BIG GAY AL
Ooh! Goodness those bullets are going

FAST!!!
Another bullet zings by his head.

BIG GAY AL
Jumping Jesus, this is insane!!
THUMP! A bullet hits Big Gay Al square in the head. More bullets follow, tearing him to shreds.

WIDE ANGLE ON - ENTIRE BATTLE
This shot parodies one of the big shots from 'Saving Private
Ryan'. Just complete overkill. Explosions, helicopters, gunfire and death.
Kyle's mother, and the other mothers as well, stand on a ridge overlooking the horrific massacre.

STAN'S MOTHER
My God... This is terrible...
Kyle's mother holds out her M-16. She is now completely insane.

KYLE'S MOTHER
This is what we wanted! We wanted our children to be brought up in a smut-free environment!!!

KENNY'S MOTHER

But we didn't want THIS. I just followed you 'cause I made a shitload of money selling Kenny t-shirts!

STAN'S MOTHER

Oh Lord, what have we done... ?

KYLE'S MOTHER

Wake up, people! We all have to do things that aren't pretty sometimes! It's the not pretty things that make life worth fighting the not pretty things for!
Why do you think children have to be born in hospitals?
The other mothers look very confused.

KYLE'S MOTHER

Why does it matter?! My plan is a perfect plan!! Perfect! Perfect! Perfect!!!!!
The other mothers walk away.

KYLE'S MOTHER

WHERE ARE YOU GOING?! We need to stop the not pretty things from letting our children be born in hospitals!

STAN'S MOTHER

We're going to find our boys! For God's sake Sheila, you almost had them killed!!
Kyle's mother turns back to the battle. More killing and explosions.

KYLE'S MOTHER

Killed. They should only be so lucky.
Kyle wasn't even BORN in a hospital!
She charges the field.

EXT. BATTLEFIELD - CONTINUOUS

Terrance and Phillip are dodging gunfire and super loud explosions.

PHILLIP

Did you hear that, Terrance? I farted!

TERRANCE

You did? Just now?
They laugh merrily.

PHILLIP

Come on, we can take shelter in one of those buildings!

But just then, Kyle's mother comes charging in with her gun!!

KYLE'S MOTHER
AAAGHGAHGHGH!!! YOU DESTROYED MY
FAMILY!!!!!!!!!!!
Phillip spins around just in time to see Kyle's mother plunge her bayonet into Terrance's abdomen.

TERRANCE
AGH!
PHILLIP
Terrance! NO!

KYLE'S MOTHER
DIE!!!!!!
SLOW MOTION SHOT -
Blood from Terrance's abdomen slowly spills from his stomach.
Everything gets SILENT as we follow the blood down, down, down...
Until it hits the ground with a huge, echoing BWOOOMMMM!!!
CLOSE UP on Kyle's mother's eyes.
CLOSE UP on the spot of blood on the ground...

BACK TO REAL TIME
Suddenly, the ground starts to open up! FWOOM!! Great flames and ash take over the sky.
Satan and his minions explode from below. Everyone stops fighting for a moment, to watch this amazing spectacle.

SATAN
RAAGHGH!!!! MY TIME HAS COME!!!
Demons and flames emerge from the ground. All the soldiers on both sides can't believe what they're seeing.
Now out of the giant abyss comes Kenny. He dusts himself off and looks around.

EXT. TRENCH - NIGHT
As more bombs and gunshots go off. Kyle, Cartman and Ike huddle close to each other in a trench.

CARTMAN
Kyle... All those times I said you were a big dumb Jew... I didn't mean it. You're not a Jew.
Kyle thinks.

KYLE
Yes I am!

IKE
Baba mama!
Another explosion rocks the trench. Dirt flies all over the boys' heads.

CARTMAN
AGH!
(Noticing Mr. Hat in his hand)
What the hell am I still holding this for?!
Cartman tosses Mr. Hat out of the trench. We hear GUNSHOTS and then VERY
FAINTLY we hear Garrison's voice.

MR. GARRISON
Mr. Hat! Noooooo!
Suddenly, Stan jumps down into the trench.

KYLE
Stan!

STAN
Dude, I found the clitoris! I think I can get Wendy to like me now!

KYLE
Sweet.

CARTMAN
(Sarcastic)
Oh, that's swell, Stan. I guess all's well that ends well, huh? We can go home now.
There's just one little thing left to tie up... WORLD WAR THREE!!!
More explosions go off. Dead bodies fly all around the boys.
Suddenly, Kenny appears before the boys.

CARTMAN/KYLE
AGAGAH!!!
CARTMAN
It's him! I told you!! Kenny's come to take us to the netherworld!

KENNY
Mph rmph rmph rmph?!

KYLE

Wait! He's not haunting us, he's trying to tell us something!

KENNY
Mph rmph rm rmph rm!

CARTMAN
Okay! We can get you some proofs of purchases for Snacky Smores Kenny! Just mellow the heck out!

EXT. SOMEWHERE IN SOUTH PARK - NIGHT
More battle. People are dying left and right.
The Doctor from the Hospital scene runs in with an M-16. A
Canadian steps in front of him, the doctor shoots, and blows the Canadian's head clean off.

DOCTOR GAUCHE
Hey, pal, don't lose your head.
Suddenly, the ticket guy's chest rips open. He falls dead, and standing behind him is a Canadian with a double barreled shotgun.

CANADIAN SOLDIER
I'm glad you got that off your chest.
Tom the Rhinoplasty surgeon leaps in and stabs the Canadian through the head with his bayonet.

TOM
I guess he got the point.
A Canadian rushes in and machine guns Tom full of holes.

CANADIAN SOLDIER 2
Plastics are a cheap and efficient insulator for electrical applications.
Just as the fighting escalates, Satan and his minions rush in.

SATAN
Yes! Good! Fight and kill one another!
The soldiers all look scared and puzzled.

SATAN
You're all part of Satan's army now!

KYLE'S MOTHER
What the hell is going on?!
Satan gets in Kyle's mother's face.

SATAN
I am the dark master!

KYLE'S MOTHER
Oh no you don't! This is MY fight!! I don't need your help, Alan Dershwitz!

SATAN
SILENCE! I AM SATAN!
KYLE'S MOTHER
Oh.

SATAN
YOU HAVE SPILLED THE BLOOD OF THE INNOCENTS. NOW THE WORLD BELONGS TO ME... NOW BEGINS TWO MILLION YEARS OF DARKNESS!! AND ALL THANKS TO YOU!!!
Kyle's mother backs down, ashamed.

CHEF
Oh, good job, Mrs. Broflofski, thanks a lot.

KYLE'S MOTHER
I... I was just trying to make the world a better place for children...

SATAN
Yes... And in doing so, you brought enough anger and intolerance to the world to allow my coming.

KYLE'S MOTHER
And I thought my mother was the master of guilt. Geez Louise.

SATAN
SILENCE!!! NOW!!! EVERYONE BOW DOWN TO ME!!!
KYLE'S MOTHER
Oh God... What have I done...
One by one, the soldiers start to kneel.
Satan throws his arms up in the air and laughs a horrible, deep laugh that fills the world.
But just then, the ground shakes again. Satan looks over to the huge abyss he had crawled out of and notices another figure.
He is burnt horribly, but it is Saddam. He holds a martini glass in his hand.

SADDAM HUSSEIN
Hey, I'm missing the party!

SATAN
No! It can't be!
Saddam, burnt to a crisp, walks over to Satan and grabs his ass.

SADDAM HUSSEIN
Did you miss me, buttercup?
(Yelling out)
All right, gang! I am your new ruler now!
Everyone bow down to ME!!
Satan puts his head down.

KYLE
HOLD EVERYTHING!!!
Kyle walks up with Cartman, Stan and Kenny.

SADDAM HUSSEIN
Oh, it's the bratty kid from hell.

KYLE
You made a deal with Kenny that if he got ten proofs of purchases from Snacky Smores you'd grant him any wish.

SADDAM HUSSEIN
And?
Kenny pulls out the proofs of purchases. TRIUMPHANT MUSIC plays.

SATAN
I TOLD you not to make that deal, Saddam!

SADDAM HUSSEIN
Who gives a fuck?! I was just fucking with him!

KYLE
What?

SADDAM HUSSEIN
The deal's off, go away, guy.

SATAN
No, Saddam. You made a deal. You can't just renege on a deal. That's lying.

SADDAM HUSSEIN

Relax bitch! You're better seen, not hear okay?
Saddam smacks Satan in the face. Now Satan looks mad, but he sits down like a good little bitch.

SADDAM HUSSEIN

Now, let's start torturing people, shall we? We'll start with...
(Looks at Cartman)
THIS little fat kid first!!

CARTMAN

AY! Don't call me fat, buttfucker-
ZAP!! A huge CHARGE shoots from Cartman, knocking one of hell's demons on his ass.

STAN

Holy shit Cartman! What was that?!

CARTMAN

How the fuck should I know!!
ZAP!!! Another huge CHARGE emits from the v-chip inside
Cartman and sends the other Swedish Soldier reeling.

KYLE

Look at that!

CHEF

It's that v-chip thing that's inside you,
Eric! The polarity must have been reversed by the electric chair!

TERRANCE

Oh boy!
A smile comes across Cartman's face.

CARTMAN
BUTTFUCKING SHIT!

BZZZZZZZZT! A huge charge busts the chains that hold
Cartman's wrists.
He jumps down.

CARTMAN

Yes!
TRIUMPHANT MUSIC plays as Cartman uses his newly found power.

SADDAM HUSSEIN

Quick, Satan! Do something!

But before Satan can do anything, Cartman holds up his hands and lets loose.

CARTMAN

FUCK A HUNK A SHIT, YOU RAT FUCK!!!

BZZZZZZZZZZAAT!!!! A charge hits Satan square between the eyes and knocks him down.

He gets to his knees and stands up again.

SADDAM HUSSEIN

Hey, you need to watch your mouth, brat!

CARTMAN

Try this on for size-

Cartman holds up his hands.

CARTMAN

DRIPPING VAGINA EATING SON OF A PIGFUCKING CRACK WHORE!!! HAIRY COCK SLURPING MAGGOT FUUUUUCK!!!! BZZZAAAAT!!

The charge hits Saddam in the chest. He drops again.

Saddam looks around and is suddenly scared. He appeals to Cartman.

SADDAM HUSSEIN

Hey buddy! No need to stress! Let me make you a deal! How about a lifetime supply of Snacky Smores and we just forget about this whole thing?!

KYLE

Don't listen to him, Cartman!

KENNY

Mrphmmmph!!!

CARTMAN

(giving in) Okay. (then) Not.

Cartman closes his eyes and hums like he's summoning up the worst words in the world. Then, it comes out. Like a volcano.

CARTMAN

**SUCK THE HOT SHIT FROM MY GURGLING ASS
YOU BLOOD DRENCHED FROZEN TAMPON ON A
STIIIIIIIIICK!!!!!!!!!!!!!
BZZZZZZZZZZZZZZATTTTTTTTT!!!!!**

A huge purple jolt emerges from each of Cartman's hands and joins into one powerful current that hits Saddam. Saddam is thrown back against the wall.

SADDAM HUSSEIN
(To Satan)
What are you waiting for, bitch?! Destroy him!!
Satan looks at Cartman, then at Saddam, and thinks...

SADDAM HUSSEIN
Come on you weak, stupid cum bucket! Save me!!
Satan stands there.

SATAN
Help you? You've destroyed my life and now you want me to help you?! You're always making me feel like a piece of shit.

SADDAM HUSSEIN
Come on guy, you know I only rib you because I love you so much!

SATAN
If you love somebody then you treat them with respect! You've never respected me!

SADDAM HUSSEIN
Can we talk about this later? Everyone is watching!

SATAN
I don't care! I want to talk about it now!
Saddam grabs Satan by the arm.

SATAN
Ow, you're hurting me!

SADDAM HUSSEIN
Listen guy, you're embarassing me in front of my friends! You know how I get mad when I get embarassed.
Satan starts getting really mad. Steam starts coming from his nostrils.

SADDAM HUSSEIN
Your little problems can wait til later, see?

Steam starts coming out of Satan's nostrils.

SADDAM HUSSEIN
Now do what I say and keep your fucking mouth shut!

SATAN
THAT'S IT! I HAVE HAD ENOUGH!!!!
Satan picks up Saddam, and throws him over a huge, flaming cliff, back into the depths of hell.

SADDAM HUSSEIN
NOOOOOOOOOOOOOoooooooooo!!!!! Heeeeyyyy guyyyyy, relaaaaaxx... . .

CHEF
Saddam Hussein is dead!

STAN AND KYLE
Hooray!!!
Everyone cheers.

PHILLIP
You're quite a purveyor of filth, little boy!

TERRANCE
Indeedy, that was a delicious choice of words!

CARTMAN
Well, I learned it all from you guys.

PHILLIP
Of course you did, cock fuck!
They all laugh merrily.
Satan stands over the cliff, looking down at where Saddam fell.

SATAN
He spent so much time convincing me I was weak and stupid that I believed it myself.
The boys look at each other, confused.

SATAN
Saddam didn't respect me. All he wanted was sex. But it took me so long to figure that out.
He starts to cry. Chef hands him a hanky.

CHEF
Here you go Satan-

SATAN
Thank you. Give me the proofs of purchases.
Kenny hands them to Satan.

SATAN
Okay Kenny, I will keep the bargain. Any wish you want is yours.
TRACK IN slowly on Kenny. MUSIC BUILDS. Finally, Kenny speaks.

KENNY
Mph rmph rmpg rmph mm.
Everyone GASPS!!

KYLE
WHAT?
STAN
Are you sure, Kenny?

SATAN
What did he say?

STAN
He said that his wish is for everyone who died in the war to come back.

CHEF
Kenny, you realize this wish is the only chance for YOU not to be dead...

KENNY
M mprh. Mph rmph rm rmph rm rmphm rmphm.
Mm rmphm rmphm rhmphm.
Triumphant music plays, as if Kenny is giving a grand, important speech.

SATAN
Very well, then. I will put an end to the war as your wish and make everything as it was
before the war started. But you
Kenny, must remain dead.

KENNY
Mph rm.
Satan turns to the open abyss.

SATAN

I must admit, I'm kind of relieved. It's too fucking cold up here.

STAN

Aren't there cold parts of hell?

SATAN

Yeah, but it's a real dry cold. Here it's the humidity that gets me. I guess I'm destined to live in hell... alone...
Sadly, Satan walks back down the trench into hell. But something catches his eye.

SATAN

Hello... What's this?
Satan bends down and picks up Mr. Hat. He looks at it, and then places it gently on his hand.

SATAN

Hi there, little guy... Would you like to go to hell with me?

SATAN (AS MR. HAT)

Sure. I bet we can be best friends!
Satan smiles. And walks down to hell with Mr. Hat.
The boys walks over to Kenny.

KYLE

Thank you, Kenny.

STAN

Yeah, thanks for going back to hell for us. You're a real pal.
A bright red light flashes and Satan and his minions are dragged back down into hell. Kenny is taken along with them.
At the same time, Garrison, Jimbo, Mackey and all the others who died, suddenly and magically appear. They look at themselves, wondering what just happened.
Everyone just stands around in a daze. Canadians and
Americans alike look at each other and wonder what to do.

MR. GARRISON

I... I'm alive... Where's Mr. Hat?

BIG GAY AL

Wow... We were all killed and now we're fine. That's super!

KYLE

Whew, I'm sure glad that's over.

STAN
Yeah, but you know, I learned something today. I learned that getting all worked up over fuck and shit and cockmaster is just stupid... You all focused so hard on erasing profanity that you forgot the most important thing... To love each other.

CARTMAN
Yeah! You're all a bunch of stupid sons a bitches!
The boys' parents walk up.

STAN
Mom, I'm a man. Just a man. And I'm going to have fun with profanity just like you and dad did when you were little.

KYLE
Yeah, so what if you say uncle raper or dicksucker or, or-

KYLE'S MOTHER
Shiteater-

STAN'S MOTHER
-Or monkey fucker-
They all laugh merrily at their naughtiness.
Wendy walks up to Stan.

WENDY
I'm sorry Stan, I guess you really DO get it after all!
Stan smiles. MUSIC swells.

STAN
Wendy... How would you like to go get some ice cream?

WENDY
Sure, Stan! How did you know I loved ice cream?

STAN
My friend the clitoris told me.

WENDY
Wow, I have a clitoris too.

STAN

138

Really? Where the hell do you keep it?
It's huge.
Wendy grabs Stan and plants a big kiss on him. Stan vomits into Wendy's mouth.

STAN
But Wendy... What about Gregory?
Gregory stands off to one side, scowling.

WENDY
Stan, I never cared for Gregory.

STAN
You didn't?

WENDY
No, dude. Fuck him. Fuck him in the ear.

STAN
Cool!

WENDY
(Singing)

Thank my lucky stars
Here before me now
Is everything I'd ever hoped for-

STAN
Knew it in a word
Saw it in a glance
The only thing I think I'd die for

STAN AND WENDY
I can't stop now... My heart's awake!
I pray your arms my arms to take!
So this is why I'm alive!
Now everyone joins hands and starts singing-

EVERYONE
SHUT YOUR FUCKING FACE, UNCLEFUCKA!
YOU'RE A COCK SUCKING ASS RAPING
UNCLEFUCKA!
YOU'RE AN UNCLEFUCKA, YES IT'S

TRUE!
NOBODY FUCKS UNCLES QUITE LIKE YOU!
UNCLEFUCKAAA!!!
Kenny's mom and dad come up.

KENNY'S DAD
This is all so wonderful. I just wish our little Kenny could see all of this joy.

KYLE
Oh he can, dude. Look!
Kyle points to the sky. Everyone looks up just in time to see a brilliant shooting star across the daytime sky.
We follow the shooting star and then slowly ZOOM in on it.
As we get closer, we realize it is actually Kenny, shooting towards the heavens.
As TRIUMPHANT MUSIC plays, Kenny's little body floats up and up through the clouds. (NOTE: This will also be done in 3-D

CGI)
Rays of light from above bathe his body and he flies up into the warmth of the baby blueness.
Angels encircle him and give him a pair of wings. They smile gently. He feels calm. He feels good.
Amidst a group of angels, Kenny flies upwards and finally... into Heaven.

END.

Made in the USA
Monee, IL
27 June 2021